Starting Points
for Reading

by Lillian Lieberman
illustrated by Marilynn Barr

Publisher: Roberta Suid
Copy Editor: Carol Whiteley
Design and Production: MGB Press
Cover Design: David Hale

Other Monday Morning publications by the author:
FolderGames for Phonics Plus,
FolderGames for Math Plus, KinderFolders for Reading Readiness,
KinderFolders for Math Readiness

Online address: MMBooks@aol.com
Web address: www.mondaymorningbooks.com

For a complete catalog, write to the address above.

ISBN#1-57612-068-6
Printed in the United States of America
9 8 7 6 5 4 3 2

CONTENTS

WORD STRUCTURE

SIGHT WORD ACTIVITIES

MINI-BOOKS

INTRODUCTION

Starting Points for Reading is a book of phonics, decoding, word structure, and reading activities for Grades 1–3. The activities are appropriate for mainstream and special education children and are ideal for use in learning centers.

The activities in the book provide starting points for building a foundation for reading, beginning with basic phonemic awareness for the perception of sounds. The skills the activities cover, which grow gradually in difficulty, include short vowels, rhyme elements, consonant blends and digraphs, vowel phonograms, basic syllable patterns, word structure, multi-syllables, and more. Activities to help the children learn words with prefixes and words with suffixes as well as sight words are provided. The carefully developed activities contain helpful reminders and cues for teacher and child.

A hands-on approach helps to make the reading activities enjoyable for children. Yarn and clothespin matches, file-folder board games including spinner games, markers, and Bingo set-ups, plus other multi-sensory activities are provided to reinforce reading skills. Icons at the top of the page indicate the type of activity for easy reference. Simple directions for making components and playing the games are included. Many of the activities can be made for individual use or made durable for extended use over time. The activities are ideal for supplementary work in the regular classroom, for special education, for individual or small group work, and for use in learning centers.

Sight word animal charts, with suggestions for use, help to reinforce needed functional sight words for beginning reading. Appealing mini-books with meaningful context complete the reading activities in ***Starting Points for Reading.***

Throughout it all, an endearing caterpillar guides and motivates the children in whimsical fashion through a series of situations—flying a kite, flipping pancakes, roller blading, playing detective. The activities make reading fun and are ideal starting points for reading!

How to Make the Activities

CONSTRUCTION

Duplicate activity set-ups. Color if desired. Glue to oak tag for durability and long-term use. Note and follow any special directions on the pages; directions within parentheses are for the teacher. Cut out parts and trim if necessary. Assemble. Glue any parts where indicated. Laminate if desired. Store loose game parts, markers, die, or any special materials in clasp manila envelopes and glue to the back of the folder or activity card. Store activities, except file folder games, in larger clasp envelopes or zip-lock bags and label. File in a box by title or skill category.

SPECIFIC DIRECTIONS

 For One- and Two-Page Activities

(Activities 1-5, 7-11, 14-17, 24-26, 29-32, 34, 36, 39, 41-42):
Follow the general directions. Make the activities for either long-term class use or for one-time individual use. For long-term use, glue the activities to oak tag for durability. For individual use, let the children construct the activities with supervision. Duplicate, cut apart, and assemble. Store in a zip-lock bag or manila envelope. Label.

 For Slip-Ins (Activities 38, 40):

Follow the general directions. Glue the activity sheets to oak tag and laminate. Cut slits on the dotted lines with a craft knife. Cut out loose activity parts. Store in a zip-lock bag or manila envelope. Label.

 For Clothespin Matches (Activities 12, 13, 33):

Follow the general directions. Duplicate activity and glue to oak tag. Cut out wheels and directions. Cut out and glue letters, words, etc., to the clothespins. Glue directions to the back of the main activity. Store clothespins and game in a large clasp envelope. Label.

For Yarn Matches (Activities 22, 28):

Follow the general directions. Glue the activity to oak tag. Cut apart except for the Footprints activity. Punch holes in the activity where indicated using the point of a pair of sharp scissors or a hole punch. Cut strands of yarn or shoestring, knotting one end. Wind tape around other end. Thread yarn through holes from the left side of the card and pull to the knot. Leave loose end free.

 For File Folder Games (Activities 6, 18–21, 23, 27, 35, 37, 43–48):

Duplicate game boards and glue to the inside center of the file folder. Glue loose game parts to oak tag and cut out. Enclose loose game parts in a clasp manila envelope and glue to the back of the file folder. Glue game illustration and playing directions to the front of the file folder. Glue game label to the file folder tab.
- **For Spinner Games** (Activities 21, 23, 43, 48): Punch a hole in each wheel. Attach spinner to wheel with brass fastener.
- **For Marker Games** (Activities 35, 46, 47): Supply markers for Hike to the Top and Prefix Parade. Provide die for Prefix Parade. For markers for The Black Hole, supply ten each of four kinds of small beans.

 For Sight Word Chart Activities (Activities 49-53):

Animal Sight Word Charts: Individual copies may be made for the children or copies may be stapled together as a set. To use, see "Enrichment Activities for Sight Words."

Sight Word Cards: Duplicate word pages and glue to oak tag. Cut apart. A solid bold line indicates the end of the words for a particular chart. Keep words in separate clasp envelopes. Glue the corresponding Animal Sight Word Chart on the front of the envelope.

 Mini-books (Activities 54-59):

Duplicate book pages. Cut apart. Make book covers by folding colored paper and cutting to size. Enclose book pages. Staple on folded side. Write the title of the book on the front cover. Children may color the illustrations.

How to Use the Activities

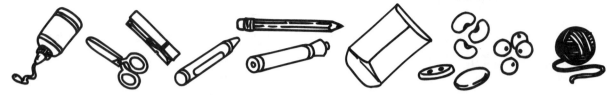

One- and Two-Page Activities: Follow the directions on the activity.

Slip-Ins: Follow the directions on the activity.

Clothespin Matches: Can be played individually or with a partner. Put clothespins face down in a pile. Pick clothespins in turn and pin to the wheels. Follow the directions on the back of the wheels. Winners are the players who find all the matches on their wheels first and read the words correctly.

Yarn Matches: Follow the directions on the activity. Children thread the yarn to the correct response.

File Folder Games (Spinner Games, Marker Games, Bingo Games, Die Games)**:** Follow the directions on the front of the file folder.

Mini-books: Use the activities in *Starting Points for Reading* to reinforce the skills needed to read the Mini-books. Go over and discuss any words beforehand that you think children may have difficulty with. A suggested list of words is provided. Select those needed and write them on the board or on paper for easy reference. Children may use the illustrations to help them with the context of the story. Have children read the books with guiding questions, such as, "What do you think will happen next?" Reread for decoding practice and expression.

Sight Word Animal Charts and Sight Word Cards: See "Enrichment Activities for Sight Words.**"**

Enrichment Activities for Sight Words

The **Sight Word Animal Charts** contain 235 functional words for the beginner reader to learn. The charts are ordered alphabetically for easy reference and are accompanied by Sight Word Cards.

Use the **Sight Word Cards** to study the words on the Elephant, Hippo, Bear, and Lion Sight Word Charts. The words can be studied with class buddies or with the teacher, aide, or an upper-grade student. They can also be worked on individually, as a class, in small groups, or one to one. When a child can successfully name the words on the cards quickly, with "one look," let the child color in the space with the word on the animal chart. Each child may have his or her own set of charts. Staple each set together and store in a manila envelope with the child's name. The file folder game "Spin the Leaf" can also be used to practice the words.

Play a Chart
Give each child the identical animal chart. Put the Sight Word Cards for that chart face down. Give each child a set of beans for markers. Then pick a card, or have the children take turns picking a card, to read and call out the sight word. (If children read and call out the words, an adult or upper-class helper could check the accuracy.) Players put a bean on the word on their chart. Then the caller spells out the word so players can check their word. If incorrect, the player must remove the bean. Set a timer for three or five minutes. When the time is up, the player with the most beans on his or her chart is the winner. There may be more than one winner. Time can be extended for older children or for children with longer attention spans. Vary the charts so that over time the children are exposed to all of the sight words.

Multi-Sensory Ways to Learn Sight Words
1. Name the word, write the word, say the word.
2. Spell and bounce a ball for each letter of the word. Say the word.
3. Spell and snap your fingers for each letter of the word. Say the word.
4. Write the word on a sand tray. Say it.
5. Place two sets of the same words face down. Pick the pairs of words.

A Handy Dictionary
Children can use the charts to look up words that they need for their stories. They can also practice their alphabetical-order skills.

Word List for Mini-books

Caterpillar Joe Goes on a Trip

big	ship	trip	best	let's	help
rush	tug	luck	rock	deck	dock
back	glad	here's	is	has	what

Caterpillar Joe's Garden

plant	rake	spade	hoe	seeds	soil
moon	high	saw	sight	grew	things
growing	store	good	said	some	you
watered	odd	funny	little	know	open
when	them				

Caterpillar Joe's Good Deed

food	smooth	boy	window	spotted	asked
started	chew	looked	around	keeper	think
thanks	cried	sadly	chairs	mister	come
can't	sure	none	would	cried	trouble
lizard	alone	picture	hamster	hey	

Caterpillar Joe Wins a Race

ready	race	triathlon	bicycle	bicycling	running
swimming	makes	takes	checks	shape	goggles
tricky	ahead	reach	long	distance	tired
more	breaks	ribbon	miles	finish	line
across	island	away	hurray		

Caterpillar Joe Solves a Mystery

morning	favorite	cereal	empty	something	nibbled
crept	hole	found	eaten	culprit	family
catch	know	clues	place	floor	mice
table	cupboards	kitchen	robber	thought	sprinkled
carefully	field	worked	flour	plenty	could

Caterpillar Joe Saves the Day

greet	free	waves	saved	crowd	Plaza Hotel
welcome	shake	piece	pocket	drawn	reaches
deed	speech	airport	wrong	motor	scooter
president	delighted	country	somehow	another	fortunately
unfortunately					

Alligator Kites

Short Vowel a

Alligator Kites

fit

rag

bet

jab

lad

vat

sad

lax

man

cut

tap

pod

Put the markers on the words with short **a** as in **alligator**. Read the words.

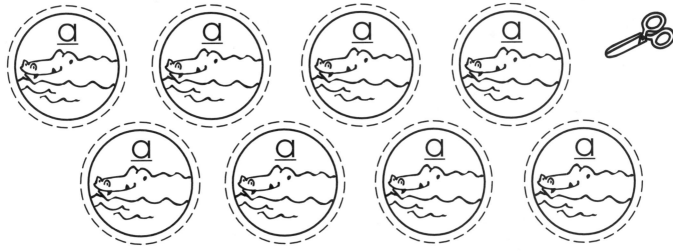

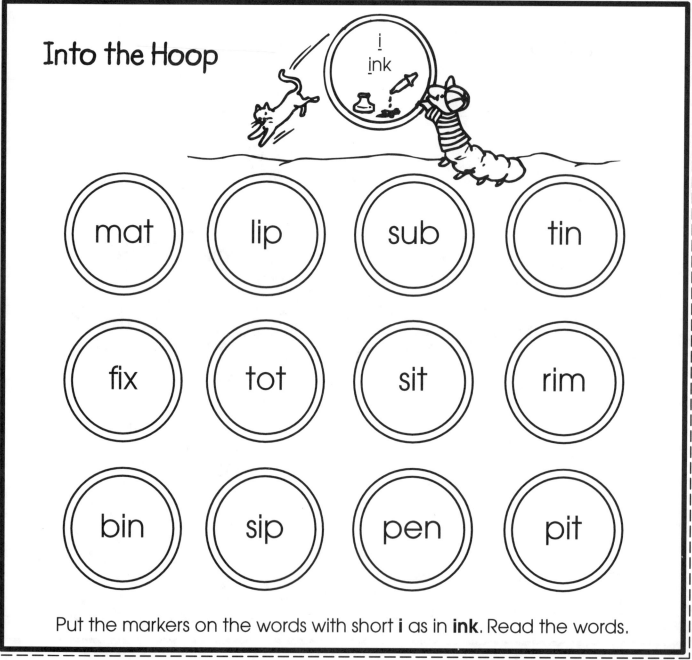

Into the Hoop

i
ink

mat	lip	sub	tin
fix	tot	sit	rim
bin	sip	pen	pit

Put the markers on the words with short **i** as in **ink**. Read the words.

Under the Umbrella

Under the Umbrella

bun	jet	cup
fin	hut	cud
tub	cod	nut
bug	ban	rum

Put the markers on the words with short **u** as in **umbrella.** Read the words.

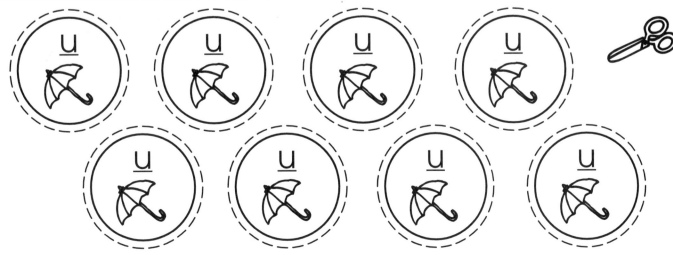

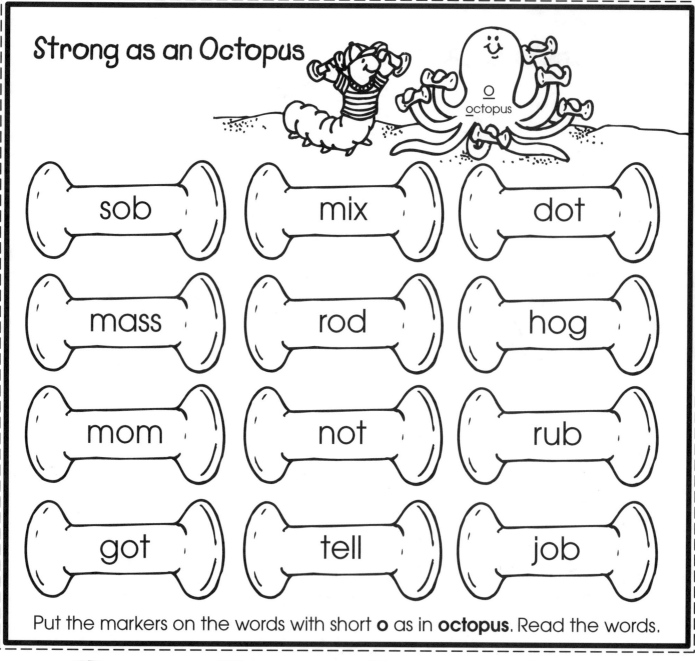

Strong as an Octopus

sob	mix	dot
mass	rod	hog
mom	not	rub
got	tell	job

Put the markers on the words with short **o** as in **octopus**. Read the words.

Elephant's Trick

Short Vowel e

Elephant's Trick

elephant

fog wet rib mess

hem tap bell leg

bed vet hug pep

Put the markers on the words with short **e** as in **elephant**. **Read** the words.

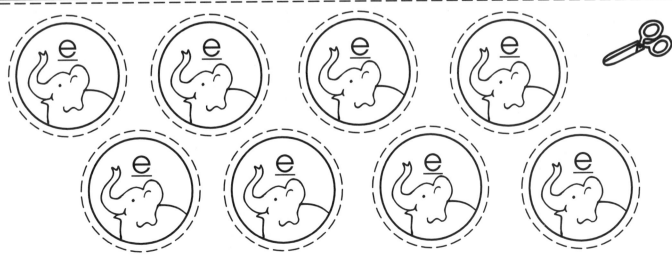

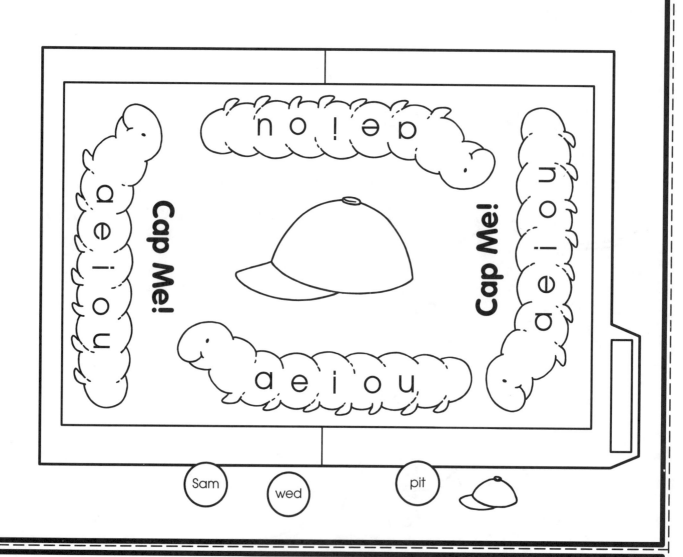

Cap Me!

Short Vowel Game

To Play:

Four can play. Choose a caterpillar to play on. Put the little caps on the big cap on the gameboard. Put the short vowel word circles face down in a pile. Take turns picking a word circle. Read the word. Put the word on the matching vowel on your caterpillar. If there is already a word on that vowel, put the word back into the pile. The player who has all the short vowel matches first is the winner. The winner puts a cap on his/her caterpillar. Play can continue until all players have caps on their caterpillars.

Cap Me!

n o

a e i o u

a e

Cap Me!

Cap Me!

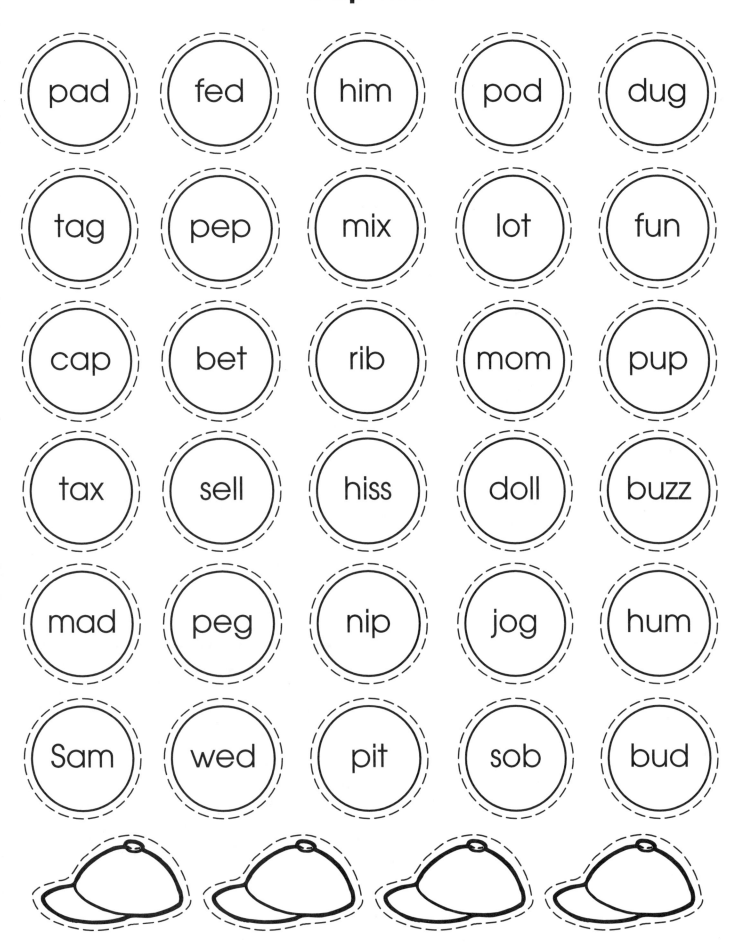

pad	fed	him	pod	dug
tag	pep	mix	lot	fun
cap	bet	rib	mom	pup
tax	sell	hiss	doll	buzz
mad	peg	nip	jog	hum
Sam	wed	pit	sob	bud

Rhyme Families: Short Vowel a

7.

Top Hat

cat
hat

rat
mat
sat

pat

tap

man

cab

wax

jam

bag

sad

Match the words with the same rhyming end. Read the words.

mad   tax   fan   nab

ham   fat   rag   map

Cupcakes

Cup Cakes

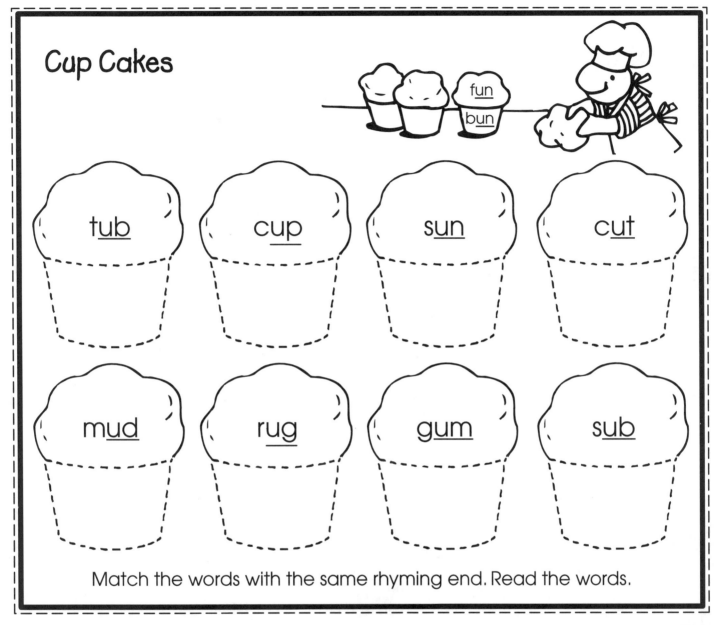

fun
bun

tub

cup

sun

cut

mud

rug

gum

sub

Match the words with the same rhyming end. Read the words.

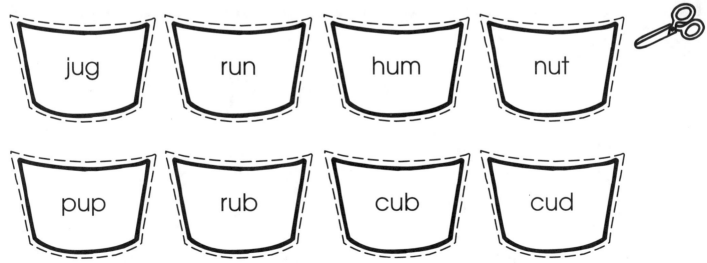

jug

run

hum

nut

pup

rub

cub

cud

Rhyme Families: Short Vowel o

Hot Cakes

jog   cot   mop   rob

cod   mom   box   son

Match the words with the same rhyming end. Read the words.

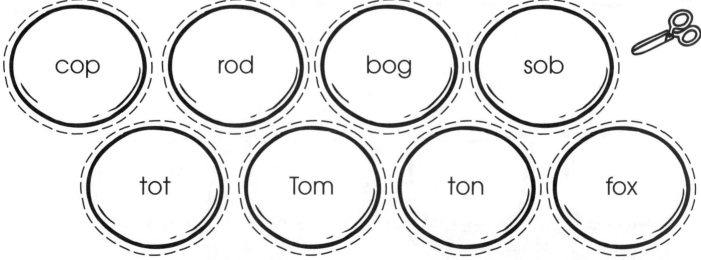

cop   rod   bog   sob

tot   Tom   ton   fox

Play to Win

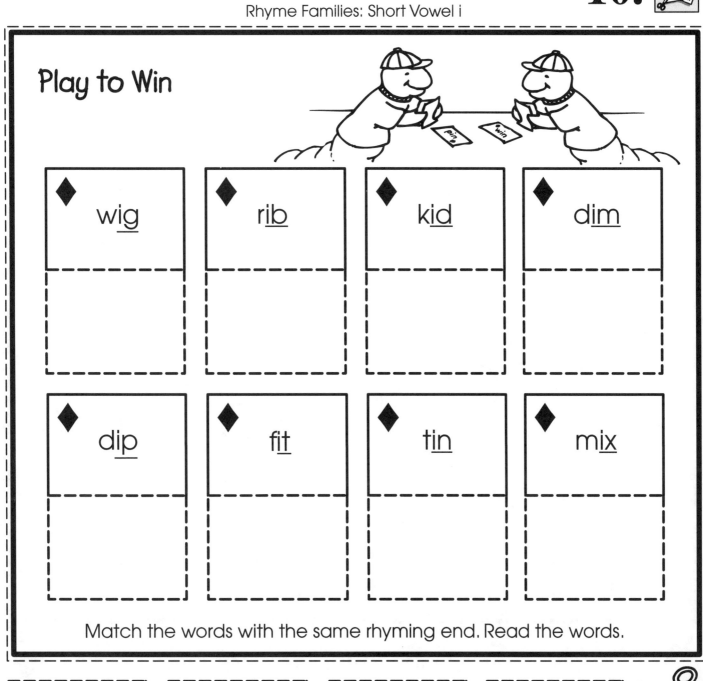

| ◆ wi<u>g</u> | ◆ ri<u>b</u> | ◆ ki<u>d</u> | ◆ di<u>m</u> |
| ◆ di<u>p</u> | ◆ fi<u>t</u> | ◆ ti<u>n</u> | ◆ mi<u>x</u> |

Match the words with the same rhyming end. Read the words.

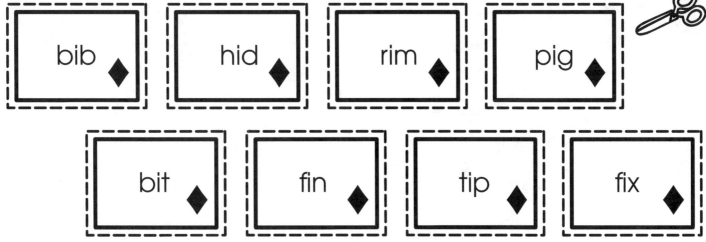

| bib ◆ | hid ◆ | rim ◆ | pig ◆ |
| bit ◆ | fin ◆ | tip ◆ | fix ◆ |

Hens on Nests

Rhyme Families: Short Vowel e

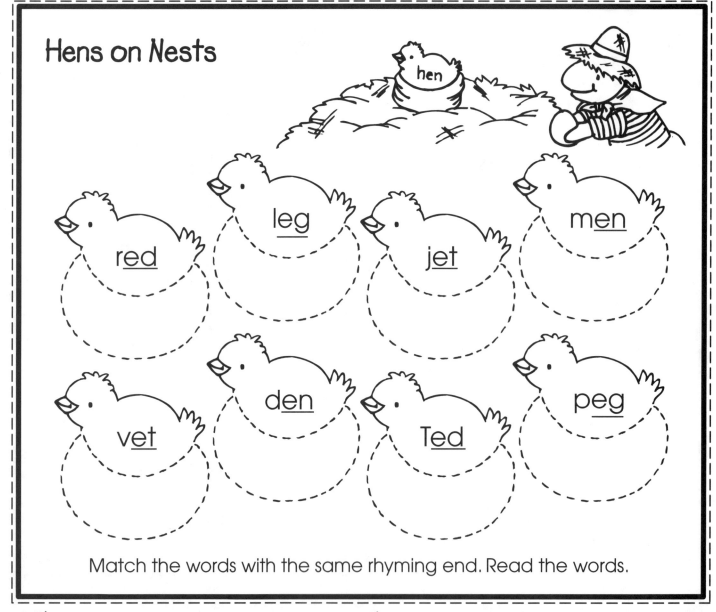

Hens on Nests

hen

red

leg

jet

men

vet

den

Ted

peg

Match the words with the same rhyming end. Read the words.

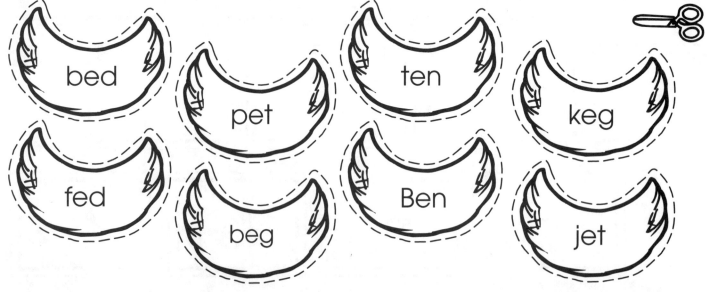

bed

pet

ten

keg

fed

beg

Ben

jet

Twin Letters

Pin the twin letters to the word. Read the word.

(Glue direction to the back of the wheel.)

Say one sound for the twin letters.

Twin Letters

lass
razz
muff
jazz
loss
puff
doll
fuzz
buzz
boss
cuff
bell
fill
dull
mess
huff

(Glue wheel to oak tag and cut out.)

(Cut apart. Glue to clothespin.)

ff	ff	ff	ff
ll	ll	ll	ll
ss	ss	ss	ss
zz	zz	zz	zz

ff

Blend Cycle

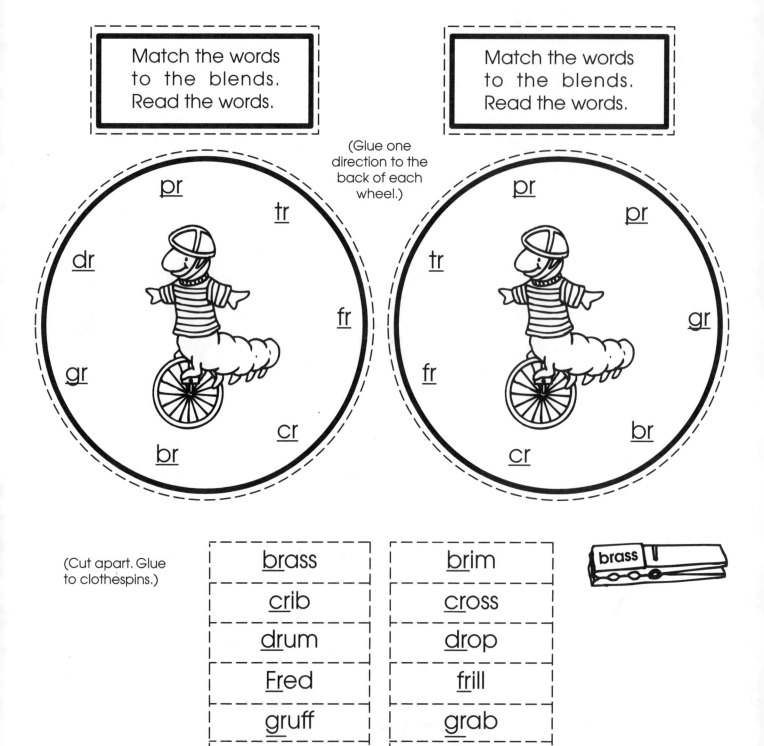

Match the words
to the blends.
Read the words.

Match the words
to the blends.
Read the words.

(Glue one
direction to the
back of each
wheel.)

pr

tr

dr

fr

gr

cr

br

pr

pr

tr

gr

fr

cr

br

(Cut apart. Glue
to clothespins.)

brass	brim
crib	cross
drum	drop
Fred	frill
gruff	grab
press	prom
trass	trap

brass

Basketball Blends

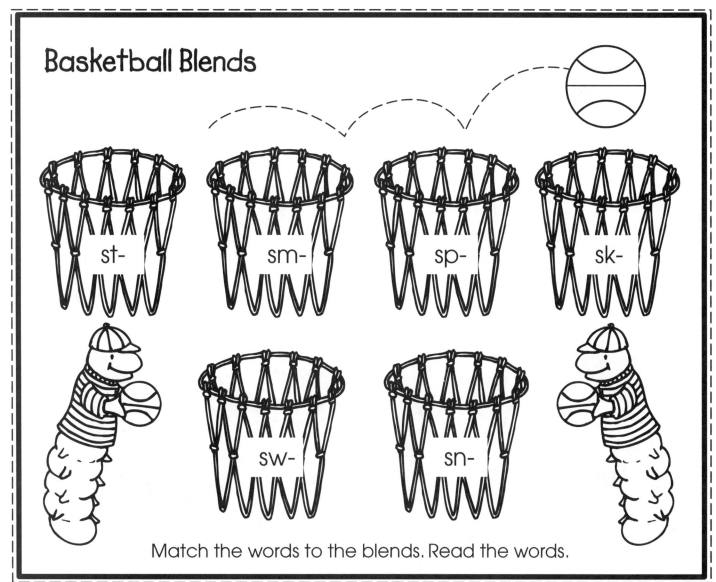

Basketball Blends

st- sm- sp- sk-

sw- sn-

Match the words to the blends. Read the words.

skin   skip   spot   spell

snap   snuff   stop   stiff

smog   smell   swim   swag

Ice Cream Scoop
Blends

___ ft   ___ lt   ___ lk

Match the words to the blends. Read the words.

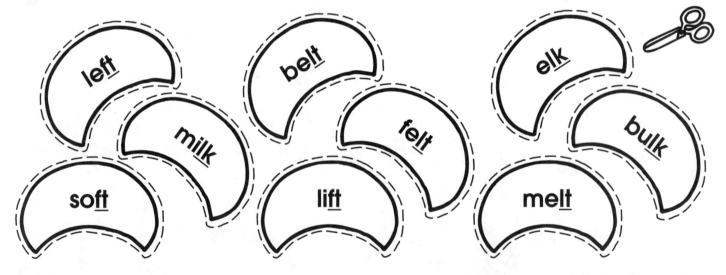

left   belt   elk

milk   felt   bulk

soft   lift   melt

Hot Air Balloon Blends

__ nd

__ nt

__ mp

Match the words to the blends. Read the words.

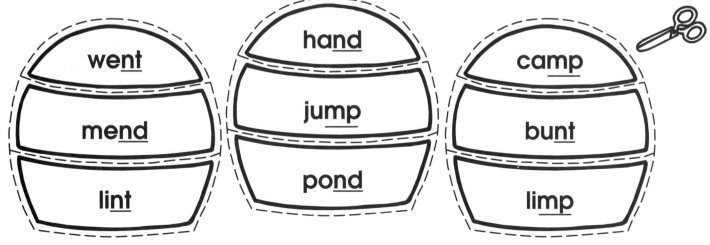

went

mend

lint

hand

jump

pond

camp

bunt

limp

Pie Blends

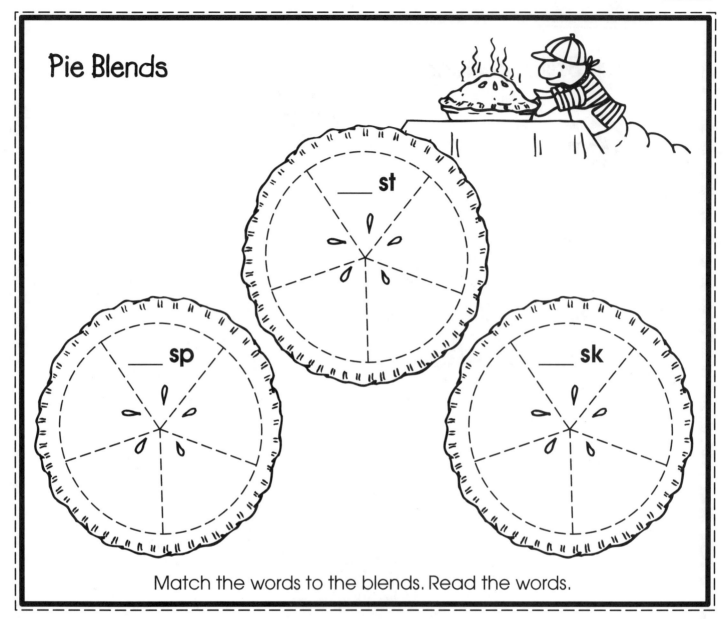

___ st

___ sp

___ sk

Match the words to the blends. Read the words.

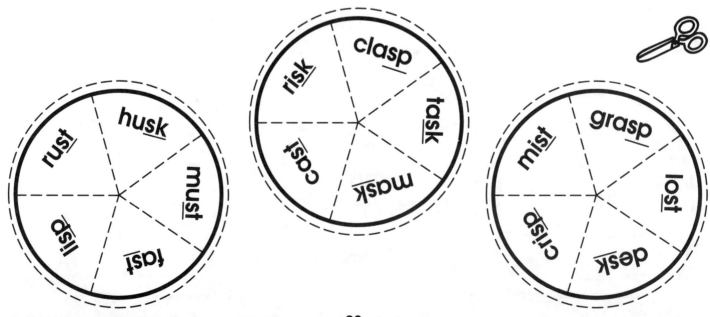

Roller Blade Blends

Initial and Final Blends

To Play:

Three can play. Set out the game with a die. Choose a roller blade marker and put it on Start. Shuffle the cards and put them face-down in the playing area. Roll the die and pick a card in turn. Read the word with the blend. If you read the word correctly, move your marker the number of spaces shown on the die. If you get a direction card, follow the direction. To get out of the traps, follow the arrow. The winner is the first player to get to The End first.

Roller Blade Blends

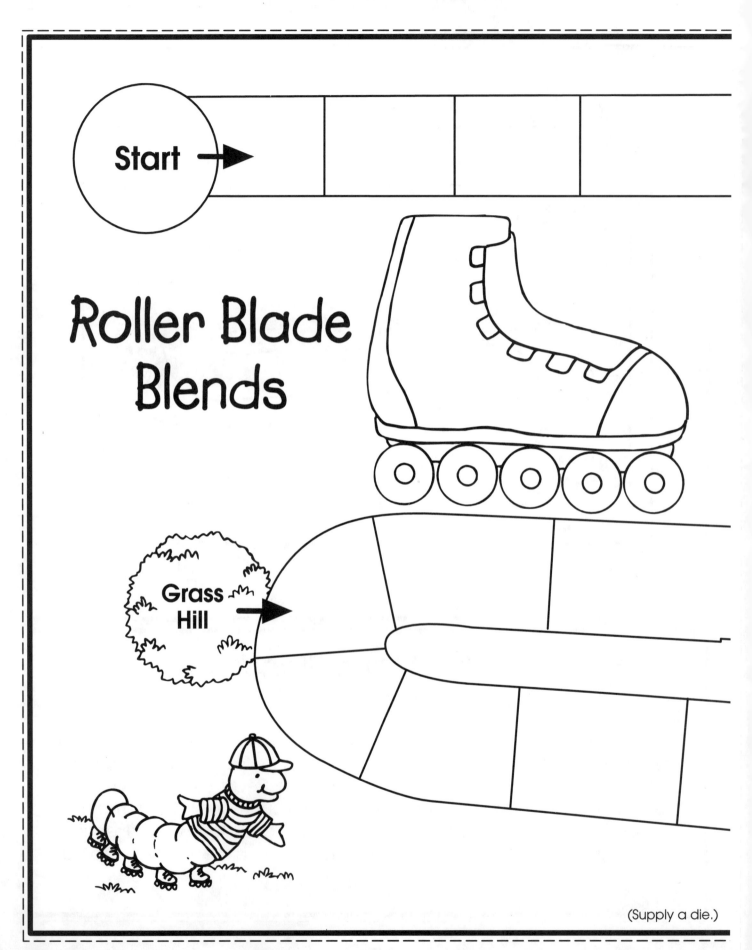

Start →

Roller Blade
Blends

Grass
Hill →

(Supply a die.)

Roller Blade Blends

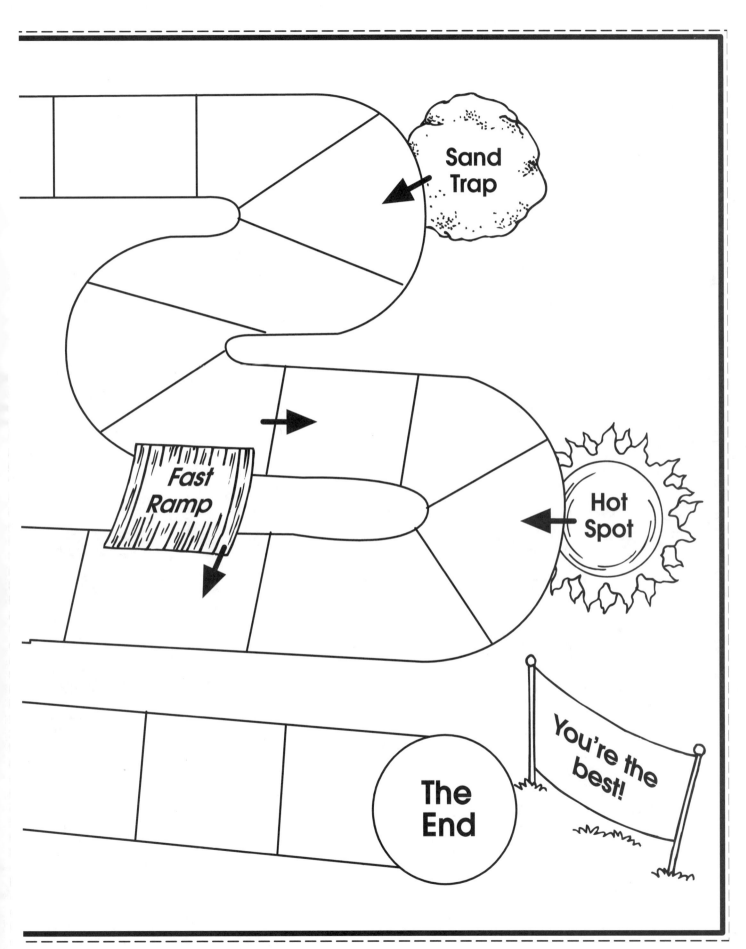

Sand Trap

Fast Ramp

Hot Spot

The End

You're the best!

Roller Blade Blends

skit	glass	prod	snip	plus
trim	smug	slot	band	spin
brad	hint	stem	crab	romp
swell	dress	best	blot	fret
wisp	clap	grip	task	flip
sulk	raft	welt	crop	gift

Roller Blade Blends

skid	drag	hulk	snub	frog
slit	grim	blip	pram	clod
trip	gloss	bond	plug	runt
swam	hump	brag	just	Skip a space.
Go back a space.	Go back to start.	Go to Hot Spot.	Go to Fast Ramp.	Go to Sand Trap.
Go to Grass Hill.	Go to Fast Ramp.	1	2	3

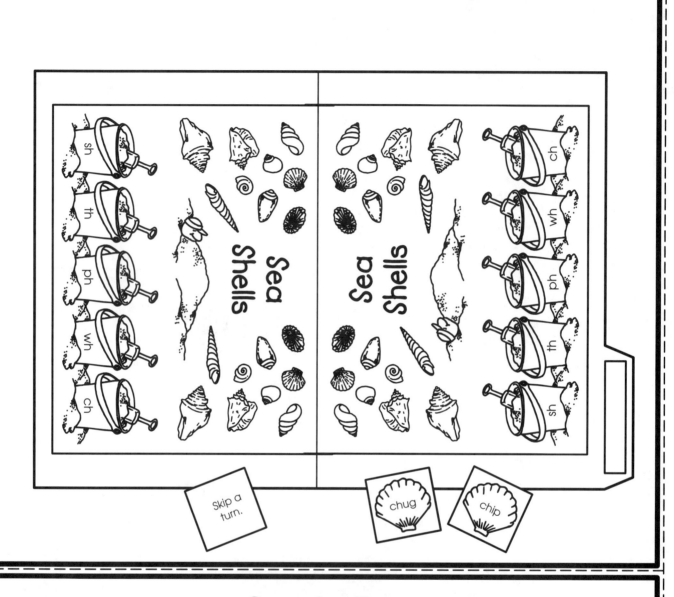

Seashells

Consonant Digraphs: sh, ch, th, wh, ph

To Play:

Two can play. Choose a side of the board to play on. Shuffle the cards and put them face down in a pile. Pick a card in turn and read the word. Put the card on the matching digraph pail—sh, ch, th, wh, or ph. If the card has a direction, follow the direction. The player who matches all of his or her digraph pails first is the winner. Reshuffle the cards if necessary.

Seashells

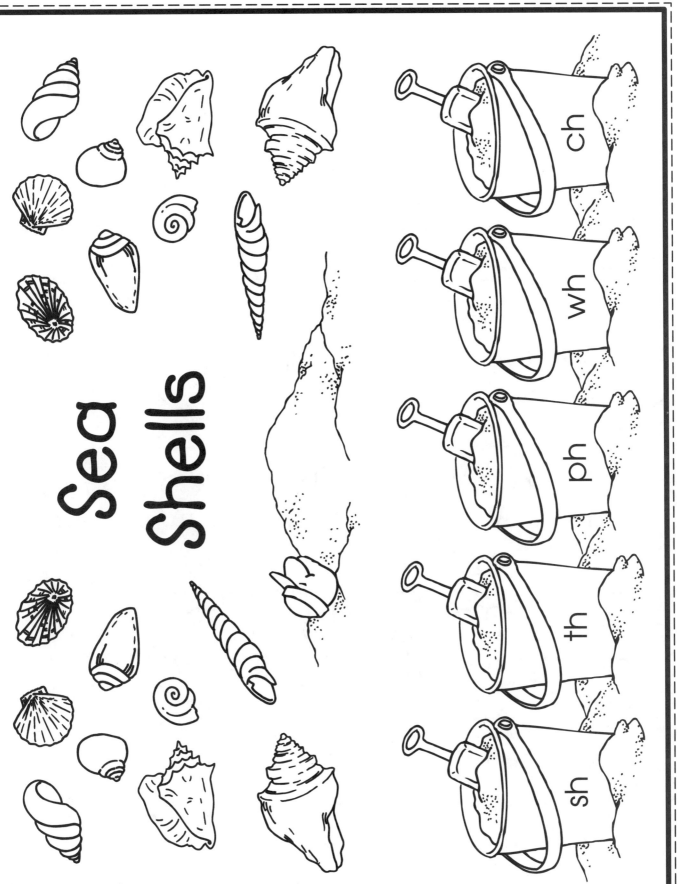

Sea Shells

ch

wh

ph

th

sh

(Make two copies.)

Seashells

chip	chug	munch	ranch	chop
shell	shag	crush	slosh	ship
than	thin	moth	them	Skip a turn.
wham	whiff	whop	whizz	Take two turns.
phone	Phil	graph	phony	Take two turns.
bath	fish	champ	whim	Skip a turn.

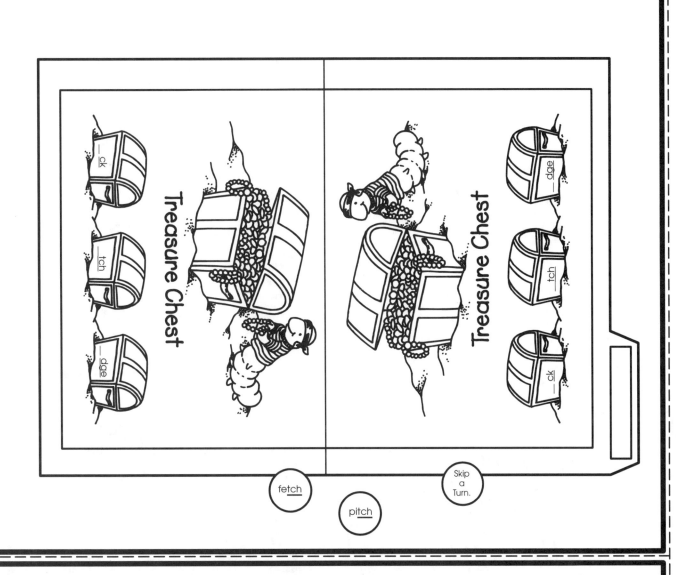

Treasure Chest

Consonant Digraph and Trigraphs: ck, tch, dge

To Play:

Two can play. Choose a side of the board to play on. Shuffle and put the coin cards face down in a pile. Pick a coin in turn and read the word. Put the coin on the matching treasure chest—ck, tch, or dge. If the coin has a direction, follow the direction. The winner is the first player to make all the matches for his or her treasure chests. Reshuffle the coin cards if necessary.

Treasure Chest

dge

tch

ck

(Make two copies.)

Treasure Chest

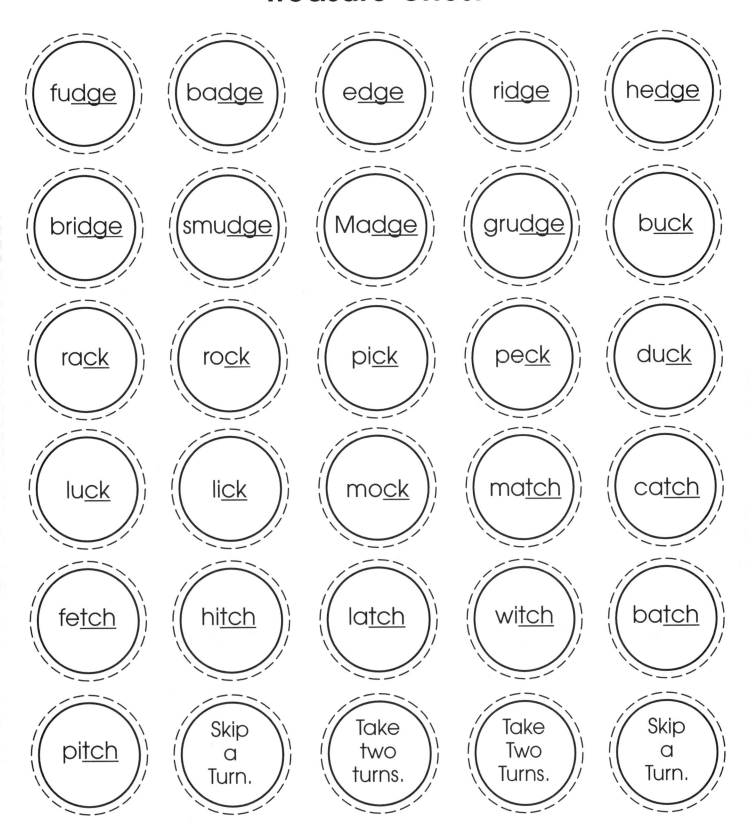

fudge

badge

edge

ridge

hedge

bridge

smudge

Madge

grudge

buck

rack

rock

pick

peck

duck

luck

lick

mock

match

catch

fetch

hitch

latch

witch

batch

pitch

Skip a Turn.

Take two turns.

Take Two Turns.

Skip a Turn.

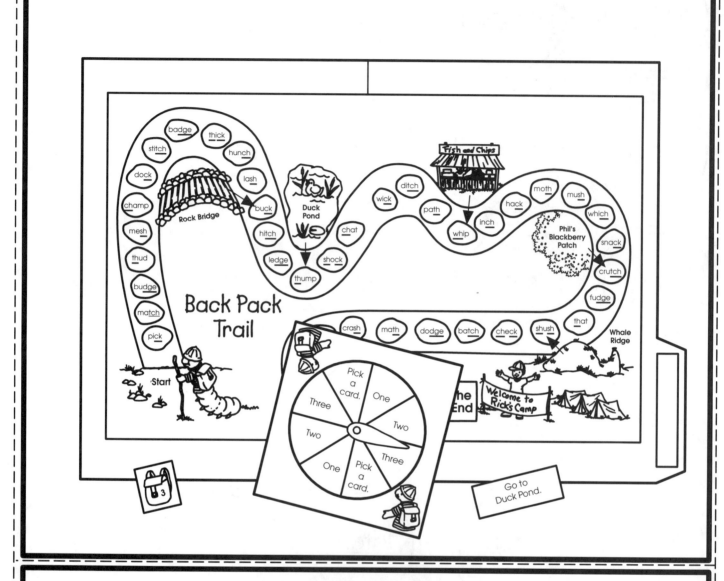

Back Pack Trail

Consonant Digraphs-Trigraphs Game

To Play:

Three can play. Set out the game. Choose a back pack marker and put it on Start. Shuffle the cards and put them face down in the playing area. Pick a card in turn. Read the word with the digraph or trigraph. If you read the word correctly, move your marker one space. If you get a direction card, follow the direction. To get out of the traps, follow the arrow. The winner is the first player to get to The End.

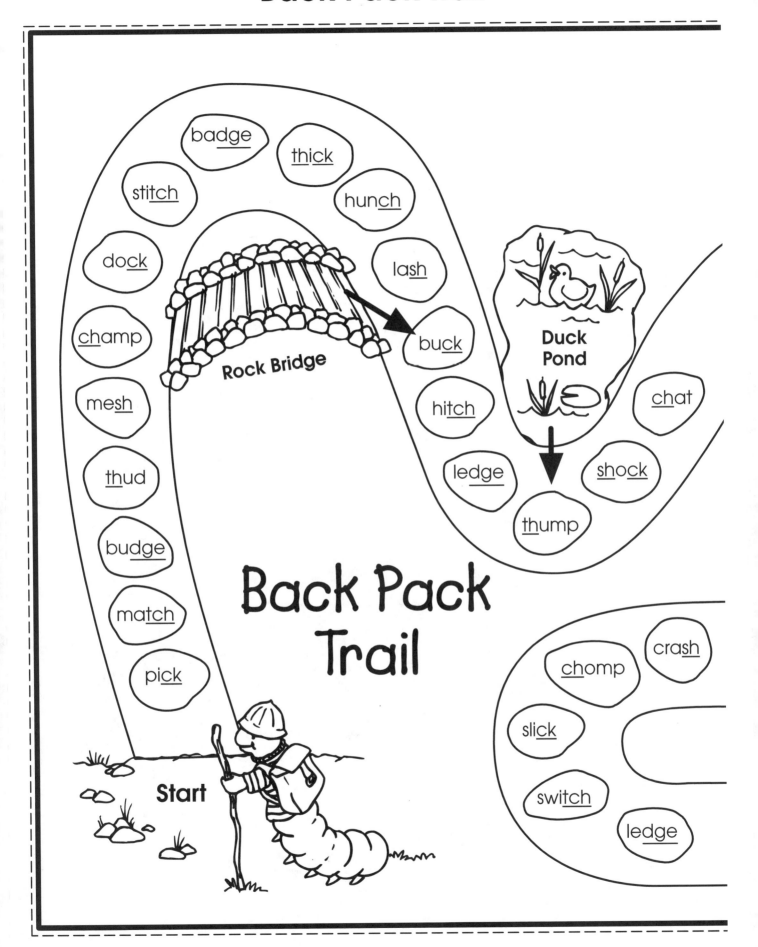

Back Pack Trail

Back Pack Trail

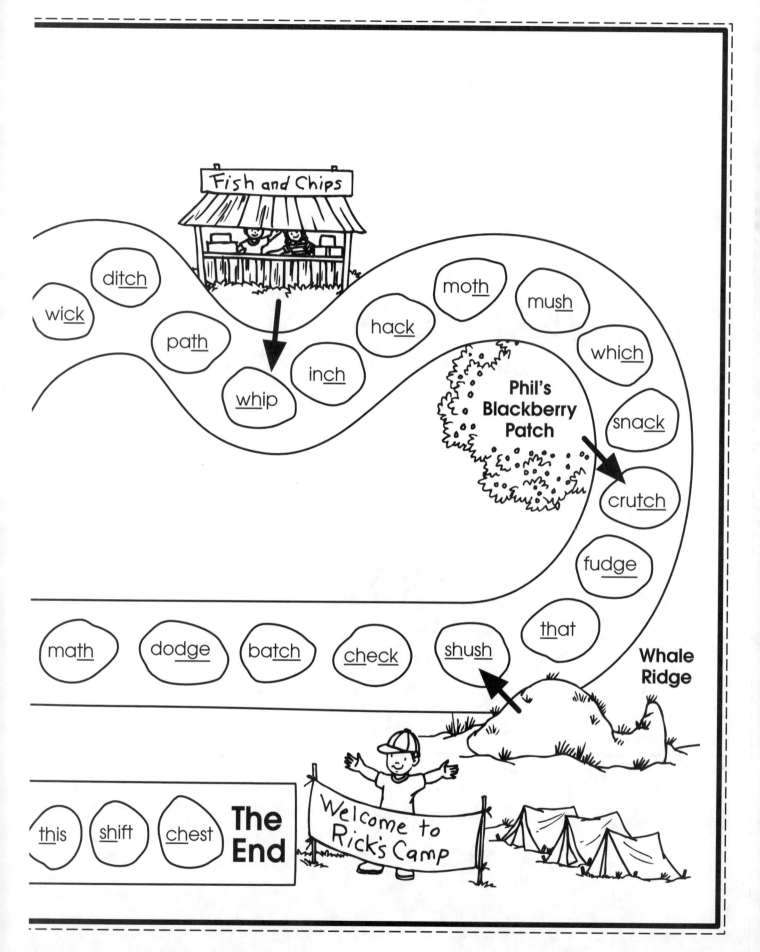

Fish and Chips

wick

ditch

path

whip

inch

hack

moth

mush

which

Phil's Blackberry Patch

snack

crutch

fudge

that

Whale Ridge

math

dodge

batch

check

shush

this

shift

chest

The End

Welcome to Rick's Camp

Back Pack Trail

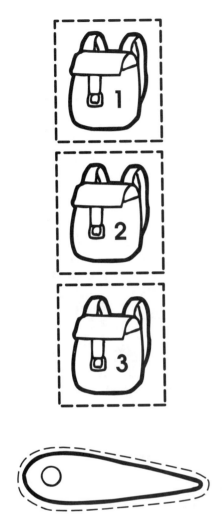

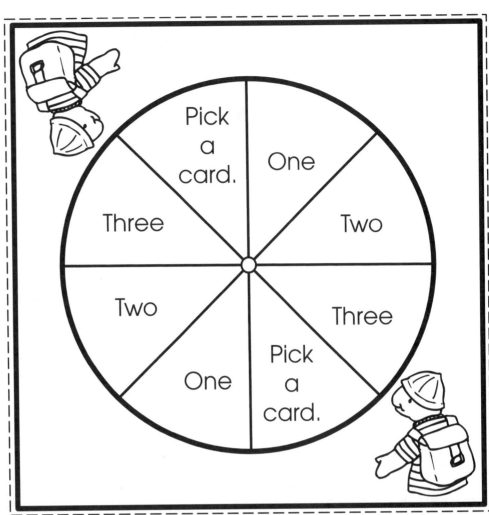

(Attach spinner to wheel with brass fastener.)

Go to Whale Ridge.	Go to Duck Pond.	Go back to start.
Go to Duck Pond.	Go to Rock Bridge.	Go to Phil's Blackberry Patch.
Go to Fish and Chips stand.	Go the Phil's Blackberry Patch.	Go to Whale Ridge.
Go back three spaces.	Go to Rock Bridge.	Go to Fish and Chips stand.

22.

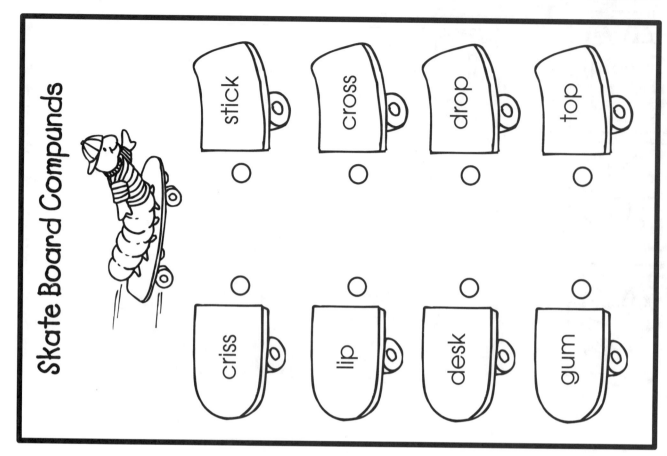

Skate Board Compunds

stick

cross

drop

top

criss

lip

desk

gum

Yarn match to make compound words.
Read the words.

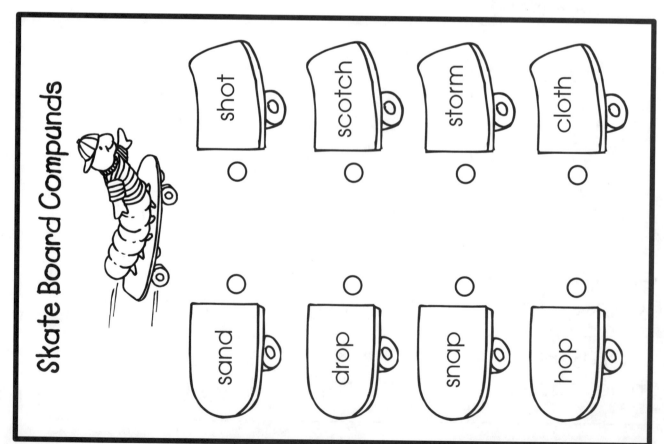

Skate Board Compunds

shot

scotch

storm

cloth

sand

drop

snap

hop

Yarn match to make compound words.
Read the words.

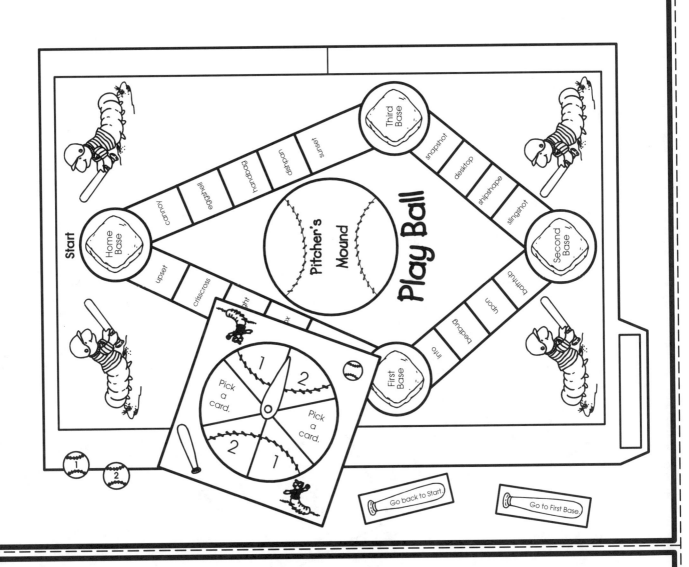

Play Ball!

Compound Words

To Play:

Two can play. Set out the game, spinner, and direction cards. Shuffle the cards and put them face down on the Pitcher's Mound. Take a ball marker. Put it on Start. Spin the spinner in turn. Move your marker the number of spaces the pointer tells you to. Read the compound word on the space. If you get a direction card, follow the direction. To get to Home Base, you must spin the exact number of spaces. The winner is the first player to get to Home Base. Or play the game three times. The winner is the person who wins two out of the three games. Shuffle the cards for each game.

Play Ball!

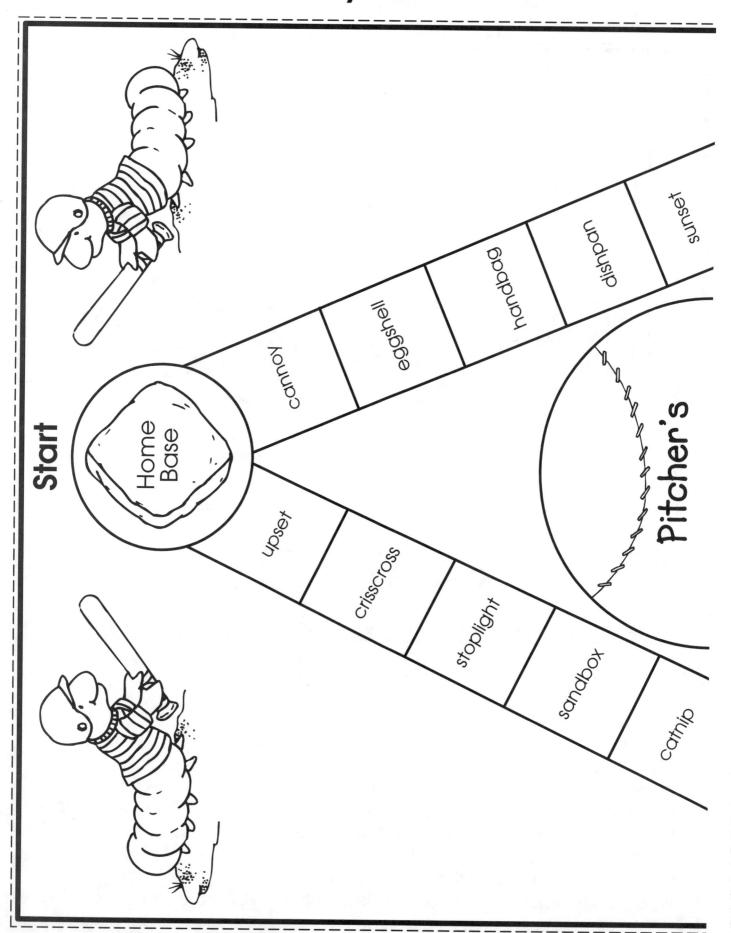

Start

Home Base

cannot

eggshell

handbag

dishpan

sunset

Pitcher's

upset

crisscross

stoplight

sandbox

catnip

Play Ball!

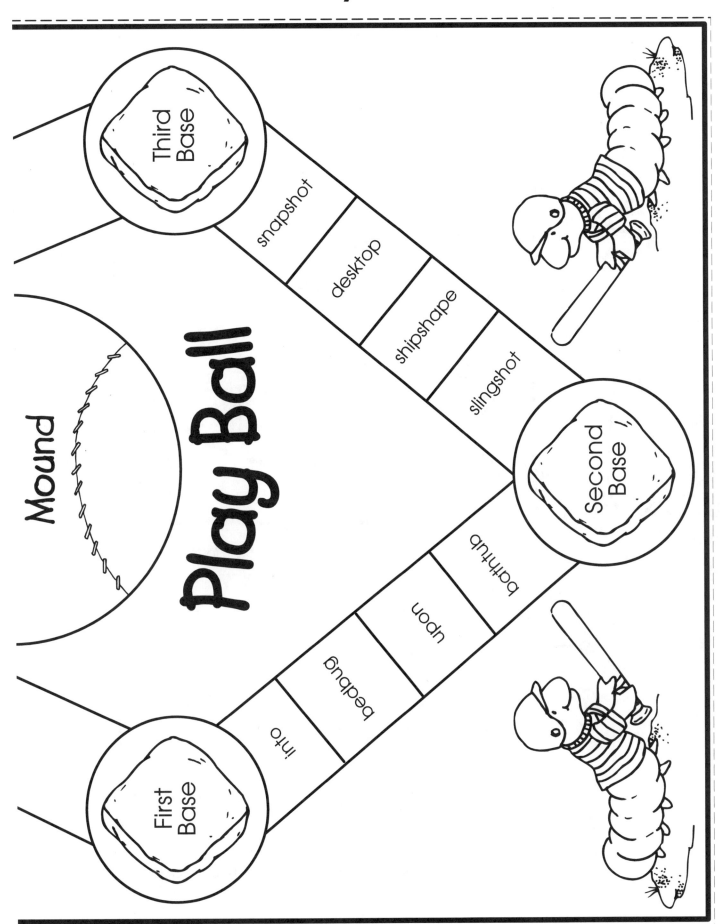

Mound

Play Ball

Third Base

snapshot

desktop

shipshape

slingshot

Second Base

bathtub

upon

bedbug

into

First Base

Play Ball!

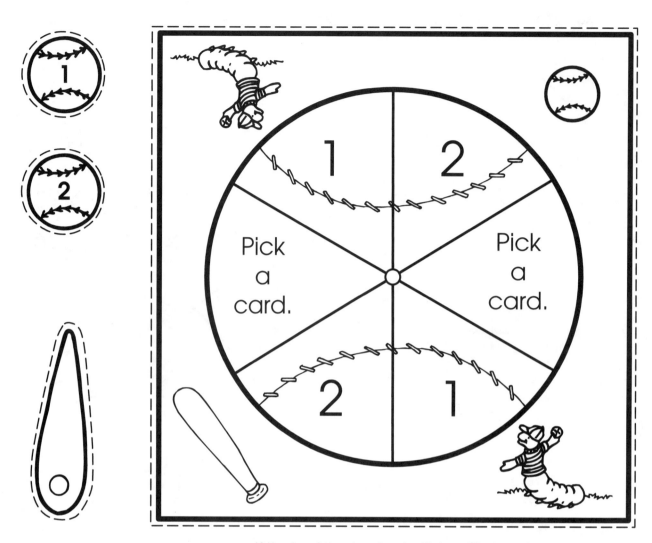

(Attach spinner to wheel with brass fastener.)

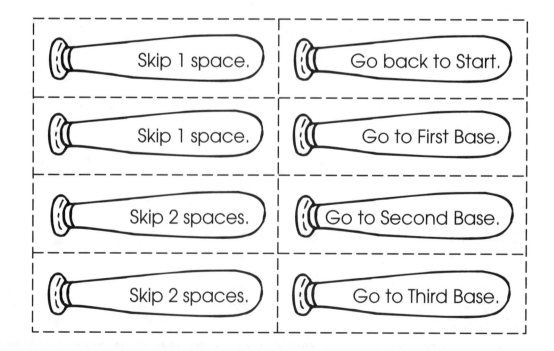

Crowns for the Kings

Letter Combinations: ing, ang, ong, ung

ung   ong   ing

ang   Crowns for the King   ang

ing   ong   ung

Cut out the crowns from the next page. Put the crowns with the matching letter combinations on the kings. Read the words.

Crowns for the Kings

spring sang song lung

bring bang long sung

wing clang tong clung

sting fang gong stung

Dunk the Doughnuts

Letter Combinations: ink, ank, onk, unk

Cut out the doughnuts from the next page. Put the doughnuts on the matching letter combinations on the cups. Read the words.

Dunk the Doughnuts

wink   tank   honk   chunk

slink   blank   zonk   hunk

blink   prank   bonk   bunk

think   crank   monk   dunk

Freight Trains

Letter Combinations: igh, eigh

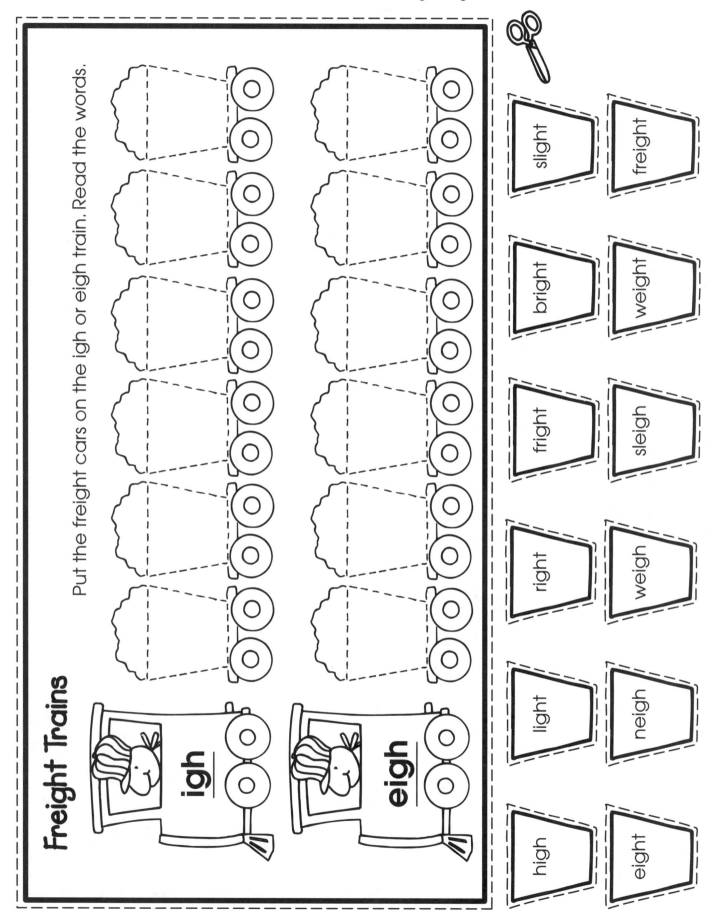

Freight Trains

Put the freight cars on the igh or eigh train. Read the words.

igh

eigh

slight

freight

bright

weight

fright

sleigh

right

weigh

light

neigh

high

eight

Double Ping-Pong

Letter Combinations Game

To Play:

Four can play. Choose a side of the Ping-Pong board to play on. Shuffle the circles and put them face down in a pile. Pick a circle in turn and read the letter combination word. Put the word on the matching letter combination space on your side of the Ping-Pong table. If the circle has a direction, follow the direction. If the space already has a word circle on it, put the word back into the pile. The first player to match all his/her letter combinations is the first winner. The team that has the most cards is the second winner. (A team is made up of the two players on the same side of the playing board.)

Double Ping-Pong

Double Ping Pong

ong eigh ang

ing ung eigh igh

ong igh ung ang ing

ing ang ung igh ong

igh eigh ung ing

ang eigh ong

(Make two copies).

Double Ping-Pong

(Make two copies).

Footprints

What is a syllable?

A syllable is a **word or part of a word** with **one vowel sound**. The word **cat** has **one vowel sound**. It is a **syllable**.

Read each word. How many **syllables** are in each word? Remember, each syllable must have **one vowel sound**. Yarn match the number of syllables to the word.

1 ○   ○ rabbit

2 ○   ○ sock

1 ○   ○ potato

3 ○   ○ coat

1 ○   ○ basket

2 ○   ○ fantastic

3 ○   ○ rain

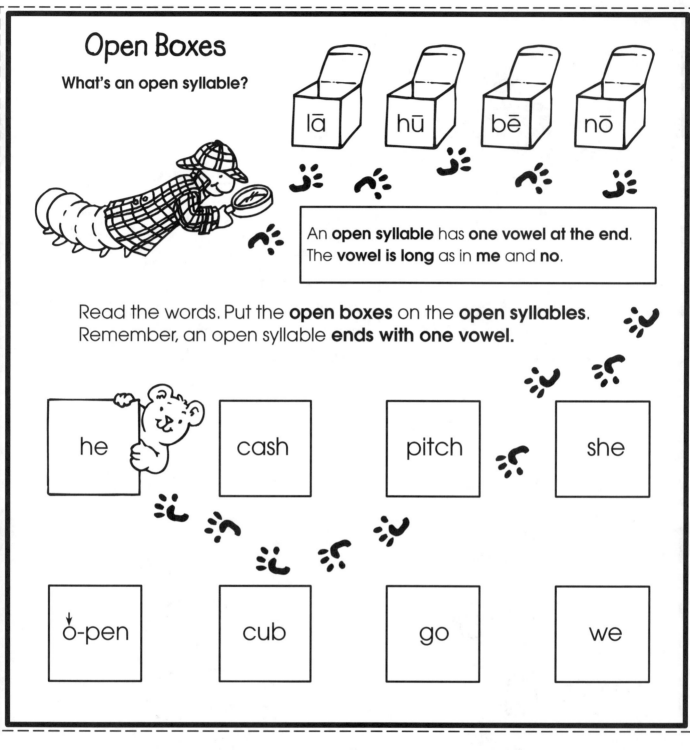

Open Boxes

What's an open syllable?

lā   hū   bē   nō

An **open syllable** has **one vowel at the end.**
The **vowel is long** as in **me** and **no.**

Read the words. Put the **open boxes** on the **open syllables.**
Remember, an open syllable **ends with one vowel.**

he	cash	pitch	she
o-pen	cub	go	we

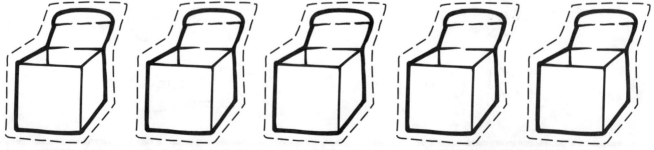

30.

Closed Doors

What's a closed syllable?

mat | pin | rent | lunch

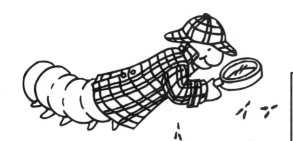

A closed **syllable** has **one vowel.** One or more **consonants** come **after** the vowel. The vowel is **short** as in **hen** and **chick.**

Read the words. Put the **closed doors** on the **closed syllables.** Remember, a **closed syllable** has **one vowel** and one or more **consonants after it**.

rat	no	rock	hi
champ	bug	be	bunch

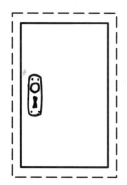 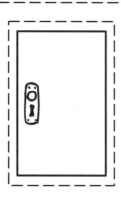 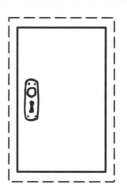 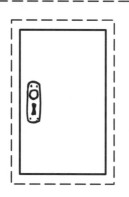 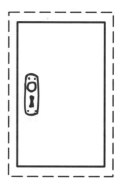

Big Bank Robbery

Open and Closed Syllables

Big Bank Robbery

Read the words.
Put the words with **open syllables** on the **open bag**.
Put the words with **closed syllables** on the **closed bag**.

Closed

Open

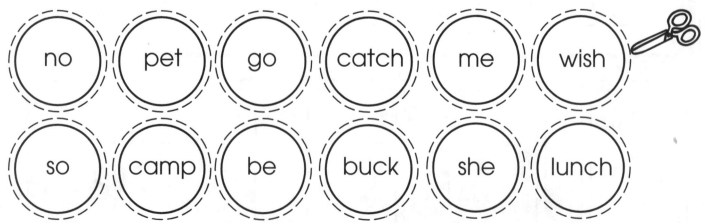

no pet go catch me wish

so camp be buck she lunch

Gold Nuggets

Gold Nuggets

What's a consonant-le syllable?

The consonant-le syllable has a **consonant** and an **-le after it**. The **dle** in can**dle** is a **consonant-le syllable**. The **e** at the end is **silent**.

Read the words.
Put a gold nugget on each word with the matching **consonant-le syllable**. Remember, it has a **consonant** and an **-le** after it.

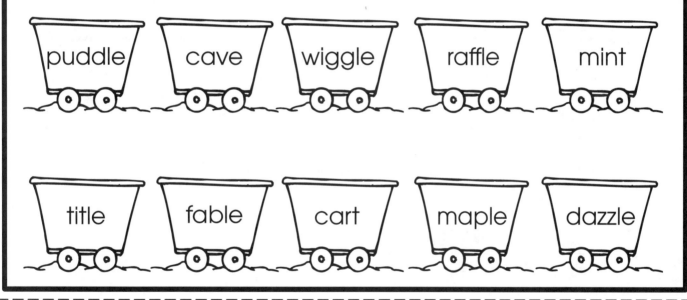

puddle	cave	wiggle	raffle	mint
title	fable	cart	maple	dazzle

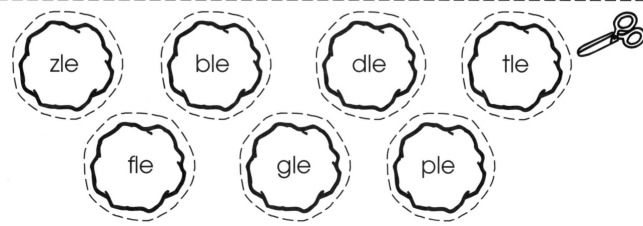

zle   ble   dle   tle

fle   gle   ple

Make a Record

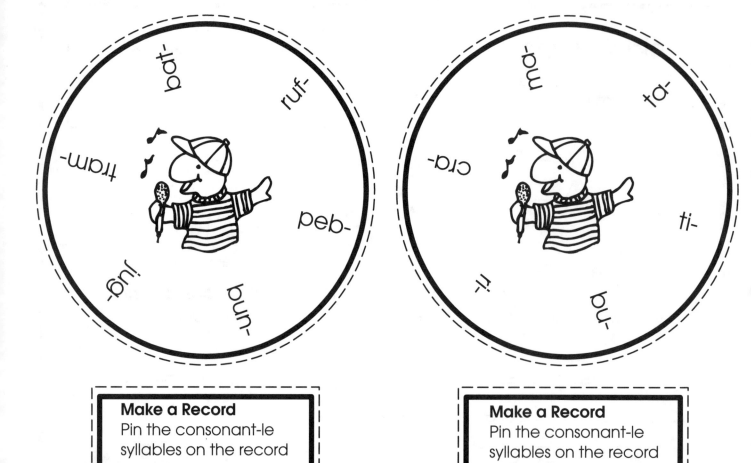

Make a Record
Pin the consonant-le
syllables on the record
to make words.

Make a Record
Pin the consonant-le
syllables on the record
to make words.

(Glue a direction to the back of each record.)

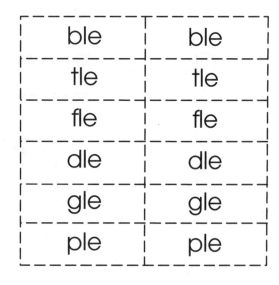

ble	ble
tle	tle
fle	fle
dle	dle
gle	gle
ple	ple

(Cut apart.
Glue each consonant-le syllable to a clothespin.)

Baby in the Buggy

What's a vowel consonant-e syllable?

The **vowel consonant-e syllable** has a **vowel** followed by a **consonant** and an **e**. The first vowel is **long**. The **e** is **silent**. <u>Kate</u> is a **vowel consonant-e** word.

Put a **silent e** on the **vowel consonant-e** words. Remember, the **first vowel is long** and the **e is silent**. Read the words.

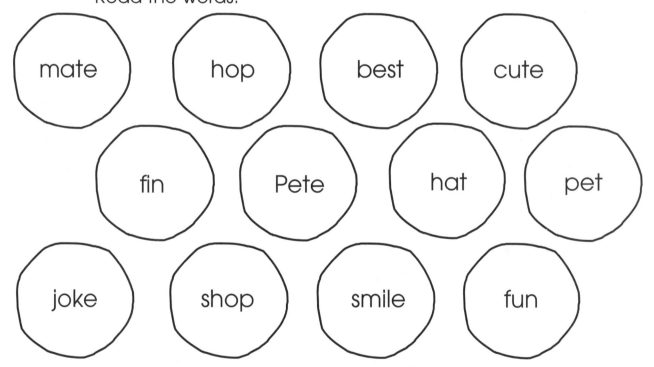

mate   hop   best   cute

fin   Pete   hat   pet

joke   shop   smile   fun

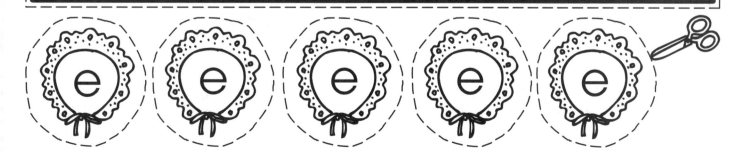

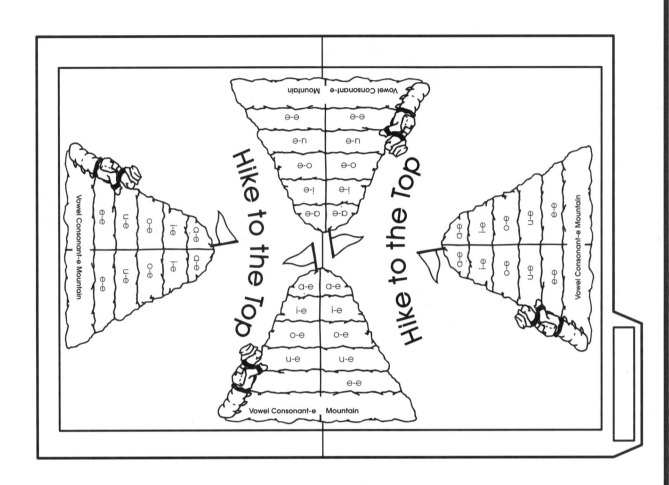

Hike to the Top

Vowel-Consonant-e Game

To Play:

Four can play. Choose a mountain to play on. Use beans or buttons as markers. Give ten markers to each player. Shuffle the word cards and put them face down in a pile. Take turns picking a card. Read the word. Put a marker on the matching vowel consonant-e pattern. For example, m<u>ake,</u> has the **a-e** pattern. If you already have a marker on the space, put the word back. The first person to have a marker on all the spaces on his or her mountain is the first winner. You can play the game three times. The player who wins two out of the three games is the Super Winner.

Hike to the Top

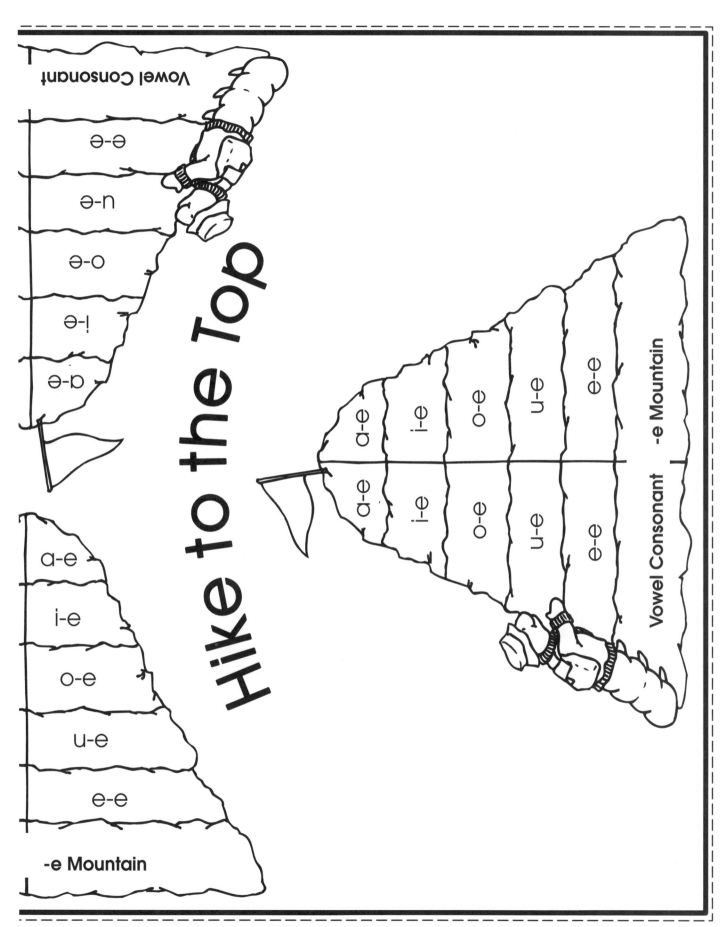

(Make two copies. Supply 40 markers, 10 for each player. Use beans or buttons.)

Starting Points for Reading • ©1999 Monday Morning Books   **67**

Hike to the Top

take	fame	shape
plane	slave	spade
pine	dime	smile
shine	tribe	slide
cone	poke	note
shown	froze	grove
mule	cube	fume
tune	duke	mute
mete	Pete	Zeke
Steve	Crete	these

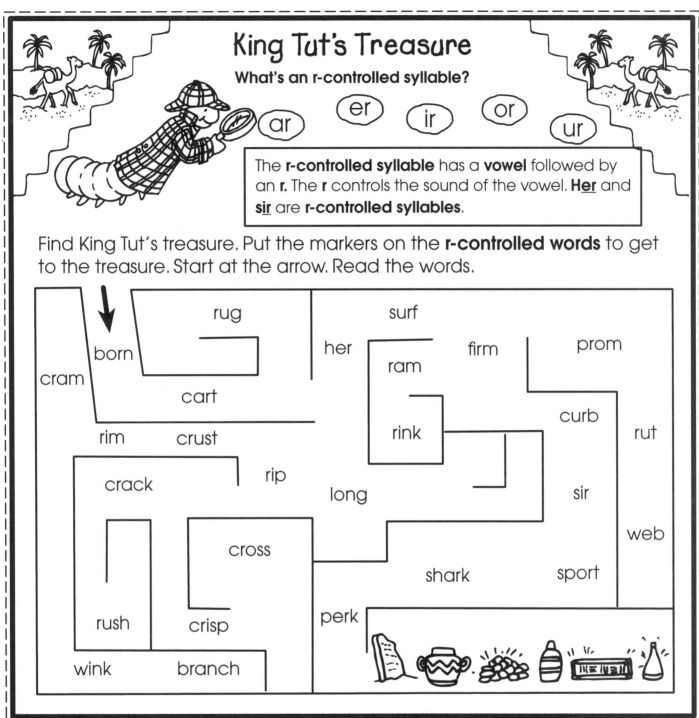

King Tut's Treasure

What's an r-controlled syllable?

ar   er   ir   or   ur

The **r-controlled syllable** has a **vowel** followed by an **r**. The **r** controls the sound of the vowel. **He̲r** and **si̲r** are **r-controlled syllables**.

Find King Tut's treasure. Put the markers on the **r-controlled words** to get to the treasure. Start at the arrow. Read the words.

rug   surf

born   her   firm   prom

ram

cram   cart

rink   curb   rut

rim   crust

rip

crack   long   sir

web

cross

shark   sport

rush   crisp

perk

wink   branch

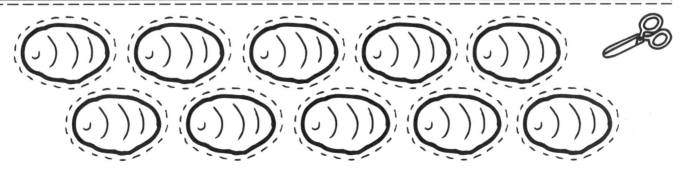

Star Bingo

R-Controlled Syllables

To Play:

Two can play. Choose a Bingo card on the game board. Shuffle the word and star cards together. Put them face down on the playing area. Take turns picking a card. If you pick a word card, read the r-controlled word. Put the card on a space under the matching label, for example, girl under the ir label. If a space is already filled, put the card back into the pile. If you pick a card with a star on it, put it on any space. To make a Bingo, fill five spaces across, down, or in a slant. The first player who makes a Bingo is the winner. The Super Winner is the first to fill all the spaces with cards.

Star BINGO

ar star	er fern	ir bird	or corn	ur purse

(Make two copies.)

Star Bingo

skirt	clerk	curl	spark	worn
girl	her	fur	start	horn
shirt	stern	turn	part	torch
whirl	herd	hurt	charm	fork
dirt	perk	churn	farm	storm
firm	perm	burst	card	sport

(Make two copies.)

Spaceships

Spaceships

What's a vowel digraph syllable?

<u>ee</u> <u>ai</u> <u>oa</u>

In a vowel digraph syllable, **two vowels** work together to **make one vowel sound**. T<u>ea</u>m, r<u>ai</u>n, and **b<u>oa</u>t** are vowel digraph syllables.

Slip the space aliens into their vowel digraph spaceships. Read the words.

<u>ea</u>

t<u>ea</u>m

r<u>ai</u>n

r<u>ai</u>n

<u>oa</u>

b<u>oa</u>t

(Glue to oak tag. Cut slits on dotted lines.)

Spaceships

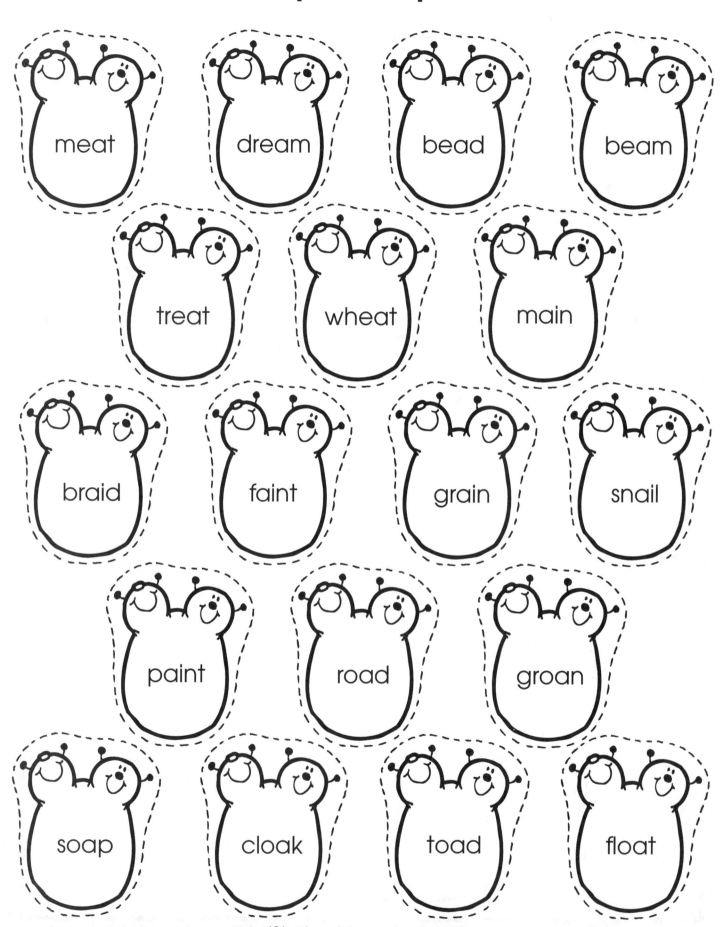

meat

dream

bead

beam

treat

wheat

main

braid

faint

grain

snail

paint

road

groan

soap

cloak

toad

float

(Glue to oak tag and cut out.)

Moon Walk

What's a vowel digraph syllable?

<u>oo</u> <u>au</u> <u>ee</u>

In a vowel digraph syllable, **two vowels** work to-gether to **make one vowel sound**. M<u>oo</u>n, P<u>au</u>l, and **b<u>ee</u>** are vowel digraph syllables.

Put the astronauts on their vowel digraph moons.
Read the words.

<u>oo</u>
m<u>oo</u>n

<u>au</u>
P<u>au</u>l

<u>ee</u>
b<u>ee</u>

(Glue to oak tag and cut out.)

Moon Walk

room

food

spoon

droop

haul

haunt

maul

launch

feel

greet

sleep

speed

Rockets in Pockets

What's a vowel digraph syllable?

<u>ou</u>   <u>ie</u>   <u>oi</u>

In a vowel digraph syllable, **two vowels** work together to **make one vowel sound**. <u>Out</u>, <u>oil</u>, and **pie** are vowel digraph syllables.

Put the rockets in their vowel digraph pockets.
Read the words.

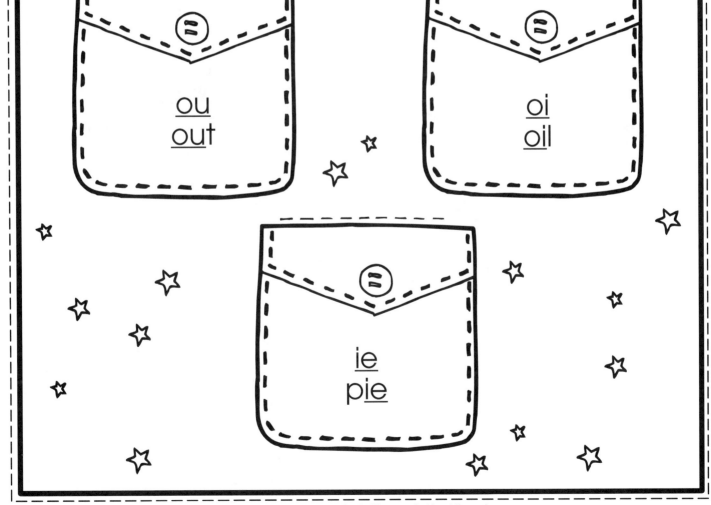

<u>ou</u>
<u>out</u>

<u>oi</u>
<u>oil</u>

<u>ie</u>
<u>pie</u>

(Glue to oak tag. Cut slits on dotted lines.)

Rockets in Pockets

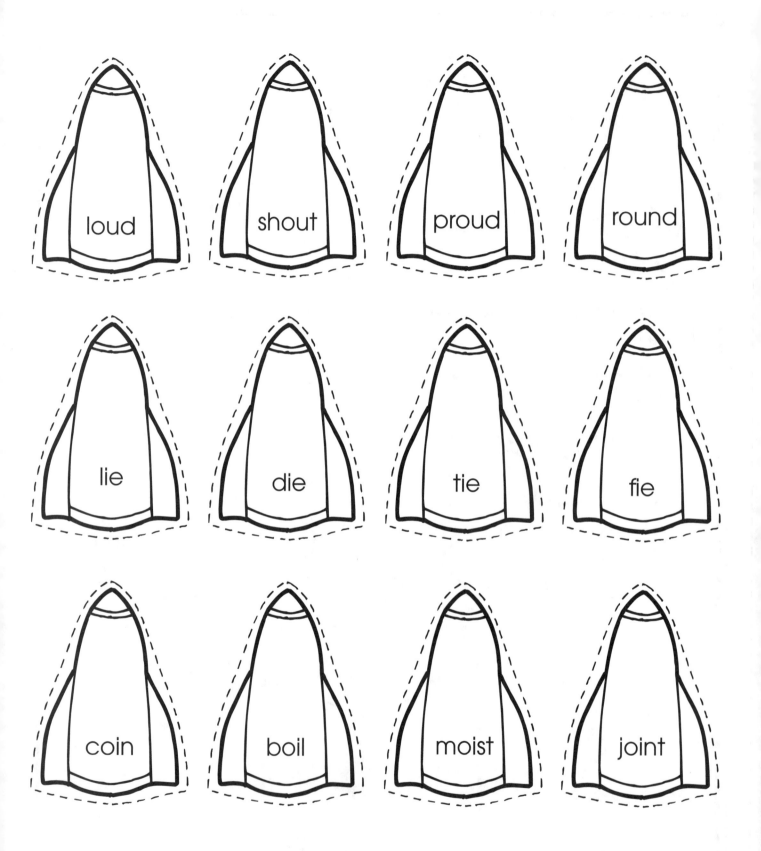

loud   shout   proud   round

lie   die   tie   fie

coin   boil   moist   joint

(Glue to oak tag and cut out.)

Sea Dive

What's a vowel digraph syllable?

<u>ay</u> <u>oy</u> <u>ey</u>

In a vowel digraph syllable, **two vowels** work together to **make one vowel sound.** In **play, b<u>oy</u>,** and **th<u>ey</u>** the **y** acts like a vowel.

Put the starfish on their vowel digraph rocks.
Read the words.

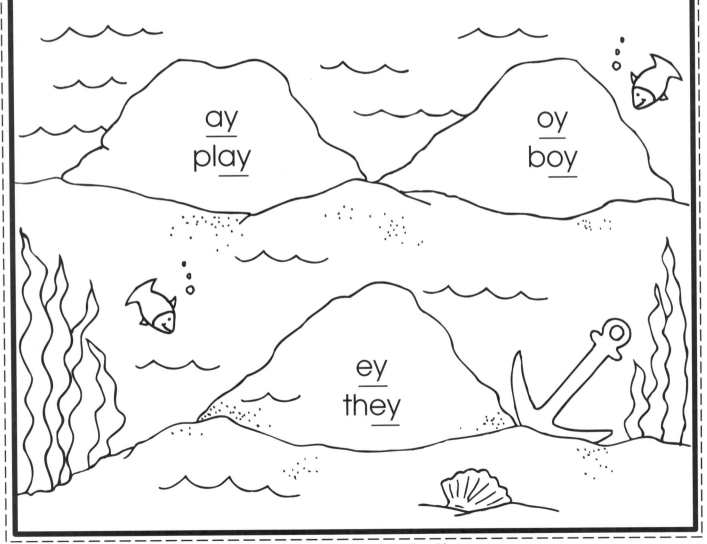

(Glue to oak tag and cut out.)

Sea Dive

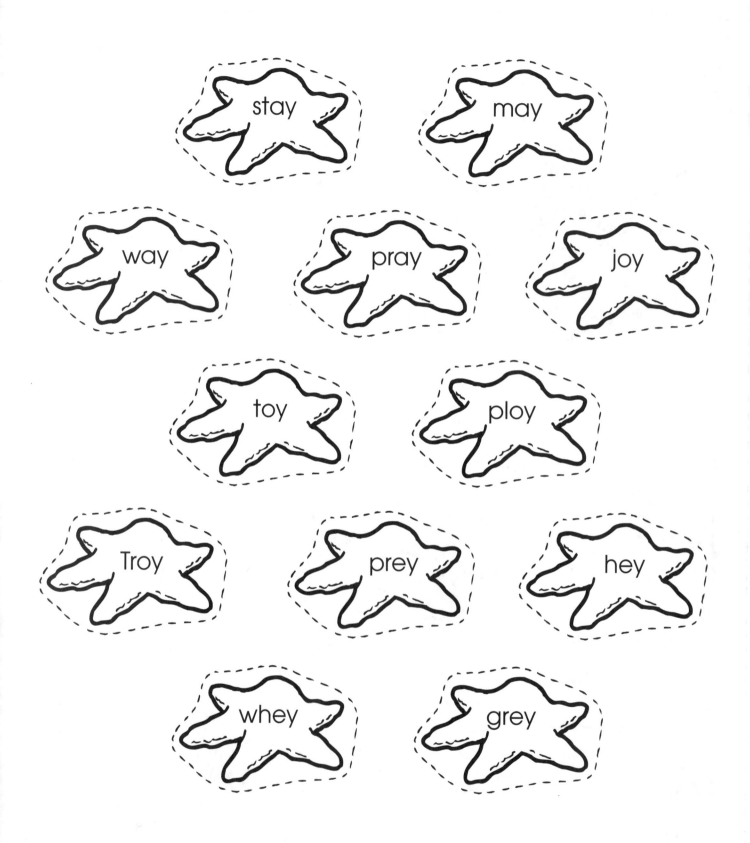

stay   may

way   pray   joy

toy   ploy

Troy   prey   hey

whey   grey

(Glue to oak tag and cut out.)

Sea Loot

What's a vowel digraph syllable?

<u>ew</u> <u>ow</u> <u>aw</u>

In a vowel digraph syllable, **two vowels** work to-gether to **make one vowel sound.** In <u>few</u>, <u>cow</u> and <u>saw</u> the <u>w</u> acts like a vowel.

Put the coins on their vowel digraph treasure chests.
Read the words.

(Glue to oak tag and cut out.)

Sea Loot

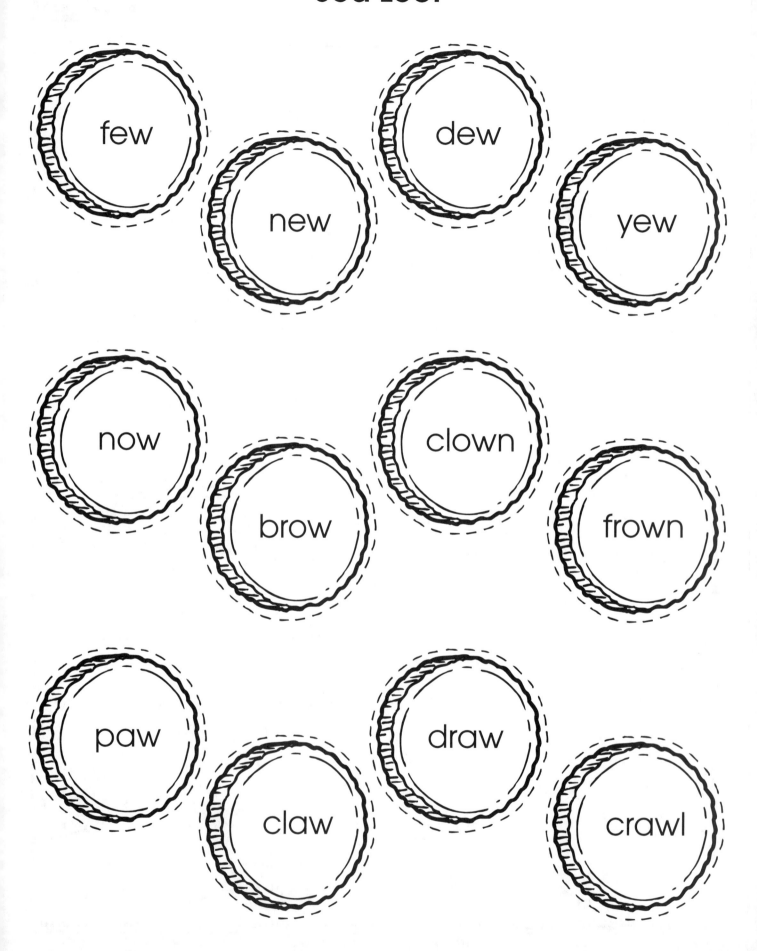

few

new

dew

yew

now

brow

clown

frown

paw

claw

draw

crawl

The Big Cheese Chase

Vowel Digraph Game

To Play:

Two can play. Set out the game board and spinner. Pick a numbered mouse marker and put it on Start. Shuffle the word cards and put them face down on the playing area. Pick a word card and and read the vowel digraph word. If correct, spin the spinner and go the number of cheese spaces the spinner tells you to. If you land on a direction, follow the direction. The player who gets to the Cheese Factory first is the winner.

The Big Cheese Chase

Start

Go back to Start

Skip three cheese.

The Big Cheese Chase

Go back one cheese.

(Attach spinner to wheel with brass fastener.)

The Big Cheese Chase

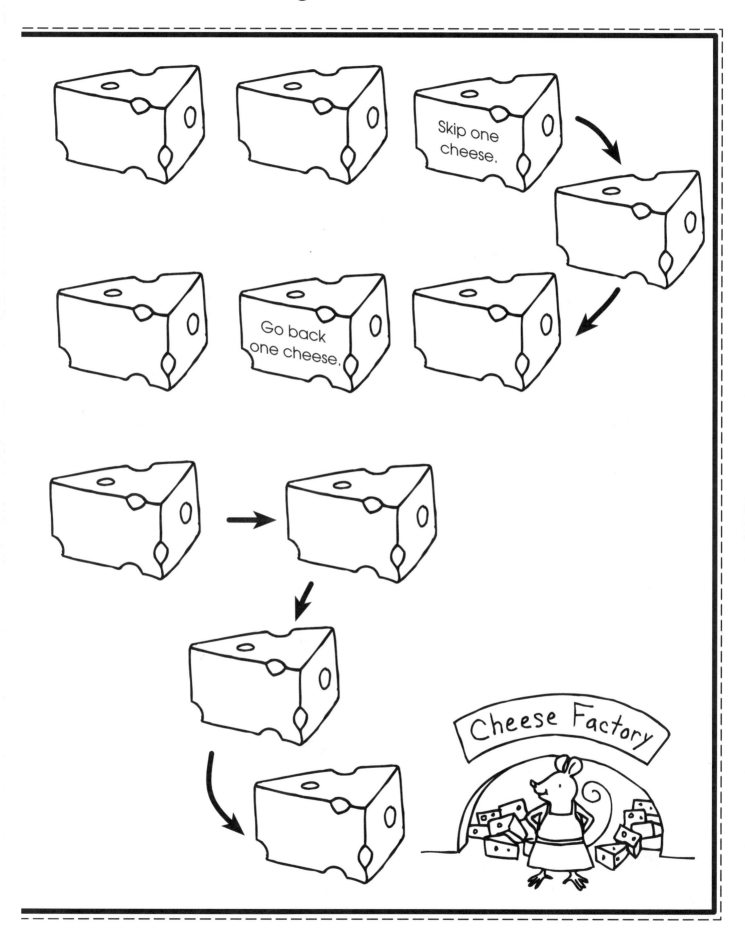

The Big Cheese Chase

spook	prey	groom	hey
haunt	few	paunch	new
sheet	howl	greed	growl
pouch	raw	stout	drawl
tie	moan	lie	toy
coil	peach	broil	dream
tray	rail	clay	train
joy	coat		

The Big Cheese Chase

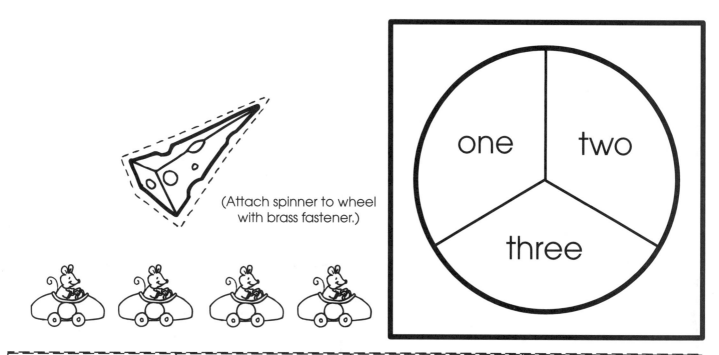

(Attach spinner to wheel with brass fastener.)

one two three

crook	stew	sweep	boy
crew	treat	round	dew
speak	slow	pie	down
crow	hoot	join	pawn
shook	Paul	sway	coach

44.

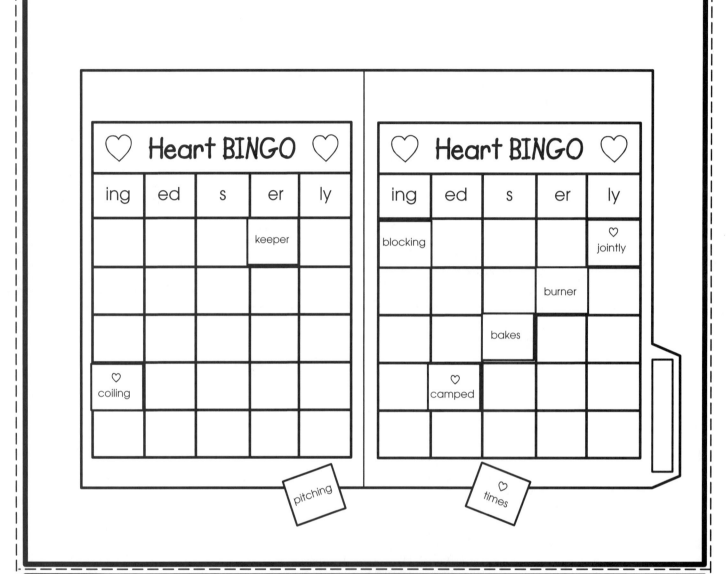

Heart Bingo

Suffixes: ing, ed, s, er, ly

To Play:

Two can play. Choose a Bingo card to play on the game board. Shuffle the word cards and place face down in the playing area. Take turns picking a word card. Read the suffixed word. If you read the word correctly, put the card on a space under the matching suffix label, for example, put block<u>ing</u>, under the <u>ing</u> label. If not correct, put the card back in the pile. If you pick a card with a heart, take another turn. To make a Bingo, fill five spaces across, down, or on a slant. If you pick a card you cannot use, put it back into the pile. The winner is the player who makes the first Bingo. You may also play to be the Super Winner—the first to fill all the spaces.

♡ Heart BINGO ♡				
ing	ed	s	er	ly

(Make two copies.)

Heart Bingo

	♡			
blocking	camped	desks	catcher	dimly
coasting	rowed	roots	♡ louder	lonely
pitching	planted	shapes	sticker	madly
crawling	started	♡ times	marker	finely
feeding	turned	bakes	keeper	♡ jointly
♡ coiling	whirled	clouds	burner	neatly
seating	sorted	claws	scooter	shortly

(Make two copies.)

45.

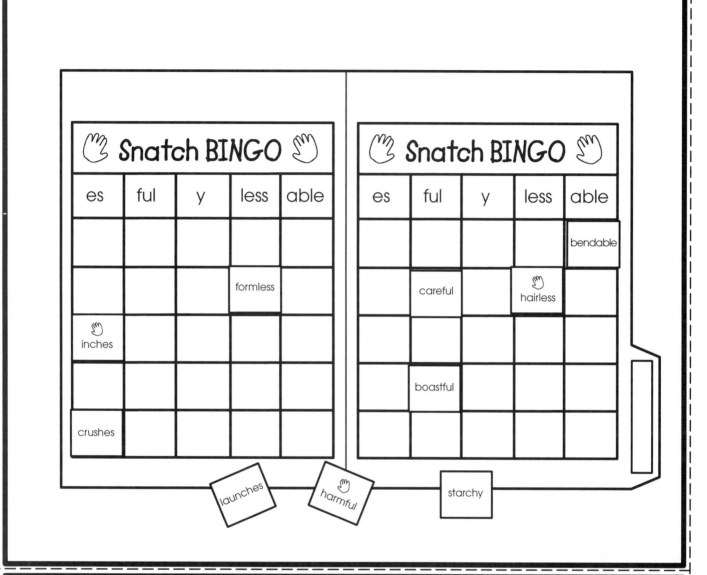

Snatch Bingo

Suffixes: es, ful, y, less, able

To Play:

Two can play. Choose a Bingo card to play on the game board. Shuffle the word cards and place face down in the playing area. Pick a card in turn. Read the suffixed word. If you read the word correctly, put the card on a space under the matching suffix label, for example, inch<u>es</u> under the <u>es</u> label. If not correct, put the card back into the pile. If the card has a hand on it, take a word card from the other player's Bingo card. To make a Bingo, fill five spaces across, down, or on a slant. If you pick a card you can't use, put it back into the pile. The winner is the first player to make a Bingo. You may also play to Super Winner by filling all the spaces.

Snatch BINGO

es	ful	y	less	able

(Make two copies.)

Snatch Bingo

patches	harmful	sporty	headless	portable
launches	careful	minty	restless	readable
inches	spoonful	roomy	hairless	bendable
marches	handful	starchy	harmless	taxable
scorches	wakeful	roasty	nameless	teachable
taxes	boastful	droopy	timeless	trainable
crushes	sinful	rainy	formless	passable

(Make two copies.)

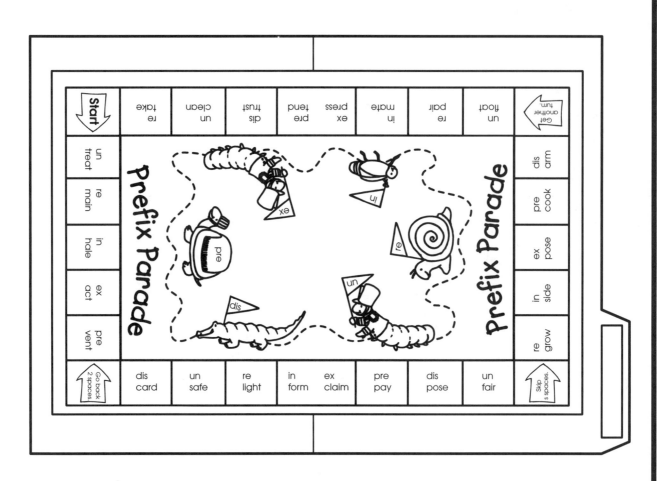

Prefix Parade

Prefix Game

To Play:

Three or four can play. Set up the game board with die and markers. (For markers, use different colored buttons, beans, or commercial markers.) Pick a marker. Put your marker on Start. Take turns throwing the die. Move your marker the number of spaces as shown on the die. Read the word with the prefix. If you land on a direction space, follow the direction. The first player to go completely around and back to the beginning is the winner.

Prefix Parade

Start ↓	re take	un clean	dis trust	pre tend
un treat				
re main				
in hale			Prefix Parade	
ex act				
pre vent				
↑ Go back 2 spaces.	dis card	un safe	re light	in form

(Supply four markers. Use beans, buttons, or commercial markers. Supply the die.)

Prefix Parade

ex press	in mate	re pair	un float

Get another turn. →

Prefix Parade

dis arm
pre cook
ex pose
in side
re grow

ex claim	pre pay	dis pose	un fair

Skip s spaces. ↑

The Black Hole

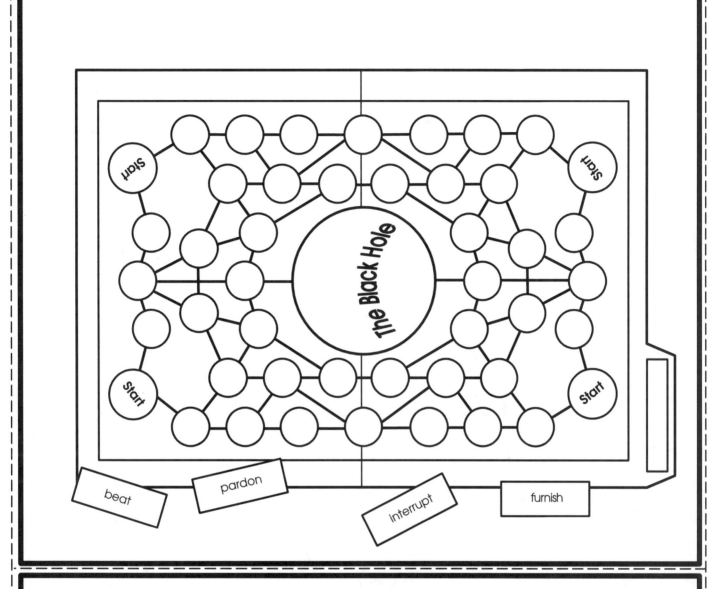

The Black Hole

Multi-syllable Game

To Play:

Four can play. Use four different kinds of beans for markers, ten of each. Each player takes ten beans of a kind and puts them in a Start circle. Shuffle the word cards and put them face down. Pick a word card in turn. Read and tell how many syllables the word has. If correct, move a bean that number of circles. Follow the lines. You may not jump circles or move into a circle occupied by another player. You can put more than one bean into play and move in any direction. Get into the Black Hole with the exact number of moves. The player who gets all his/her beans into the Black Hole first is the winner. Reuse cards if needed.

The Black Hole

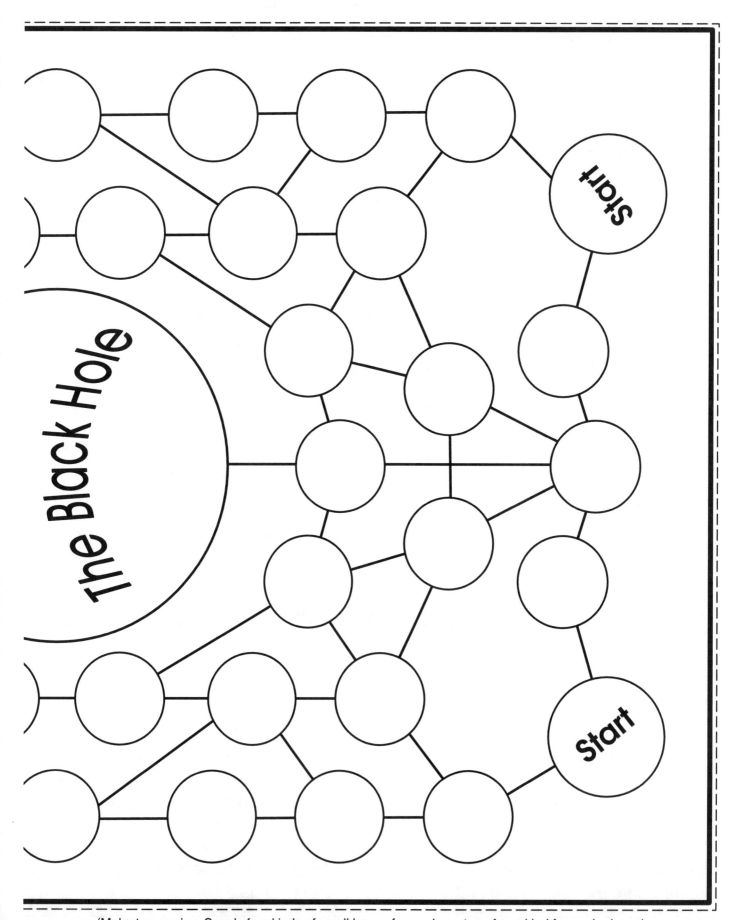

(Make two copies. Supply four kinds of small beans for markers, ten of one kind for each player.)

The Black Hole

beat	window	contentment
choke	pardon	remember
bread	fable	interrupt
crown	sample	important
hound	furnish	hamburger
sight	whisper	concentrate
launch	checkmate	tornado
snail	plastic	telescope
churn	demon	lemonade
branch	tenant	lollipop

(Make two copies.)

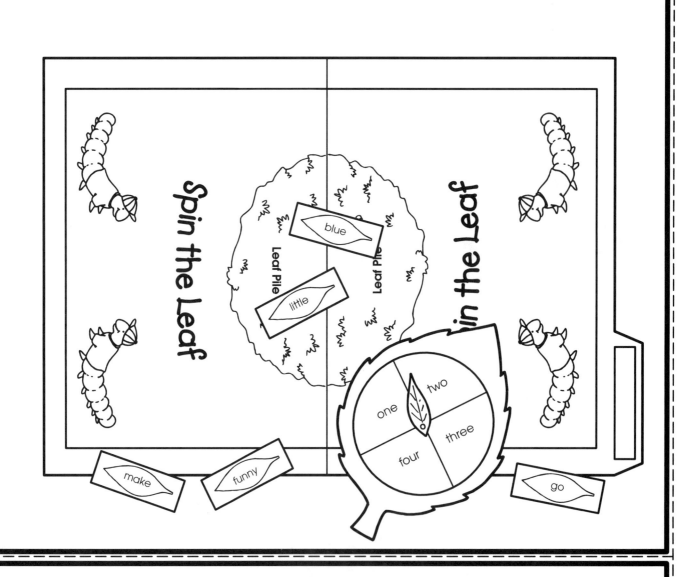

Spin the Leaf

Sight Word Game

To Play:

Four can play. Set up the game board with the spinner and leaf word cards. Choose a caterpillar to play on. Put the leaf word cards face down in the Leaf Pile circle. Spin the spinner in turn. Pick as many leaves as the pointer tells you to. Read the words and show the cards so other players can check for correctness. Put all correctly read words on your caterpillar. Put back the words you need more help with. The winner is the player with the most leaves.

Leaf Pile

Spin the Leaf

(Make two copies.)

Spin the Leaf

(Attach spinner to wheel with brass fastener.)

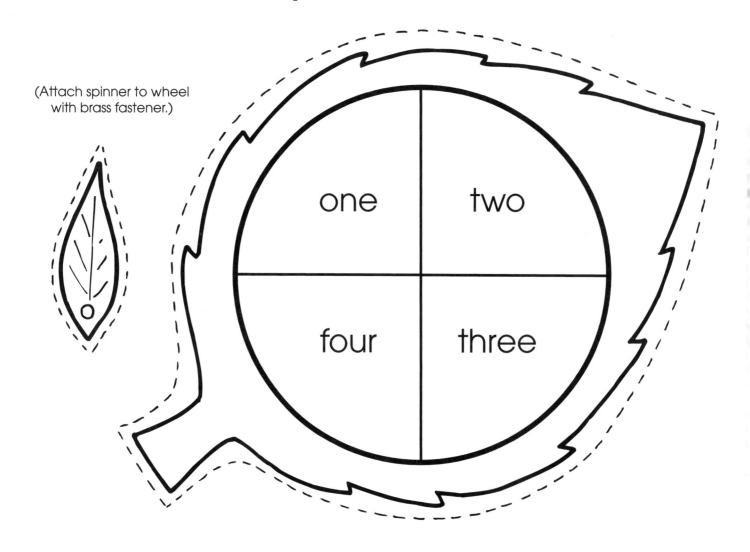

one | two

four | three

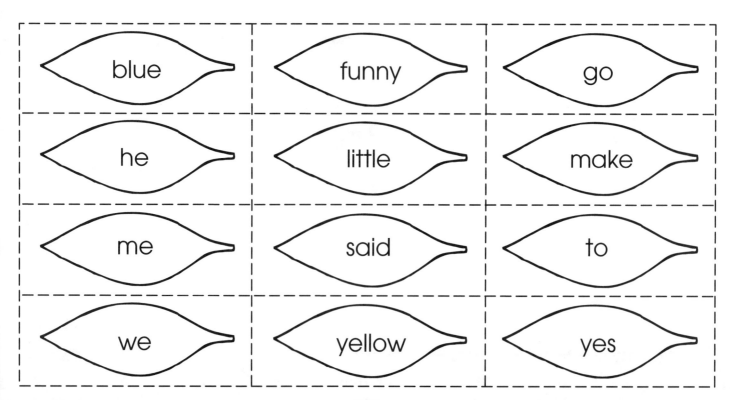

blue

funny

go

he

little

make

me

said

to

we

yellow

yes

Spin the Leaf

my	brown	zoo
ride	look	come
see	you	was
have	good	play
down	four	two
jump	now	an
am	red	by
big	at	are
I	in	is

Spin the Leaf

like	saw	too
black	do	no
put	say	so
with	will	well
five	find	for
here	white	this
she	they	has
that	the	what
his	some	of

Elephant Words
(Sight Word Chart 1)

49.

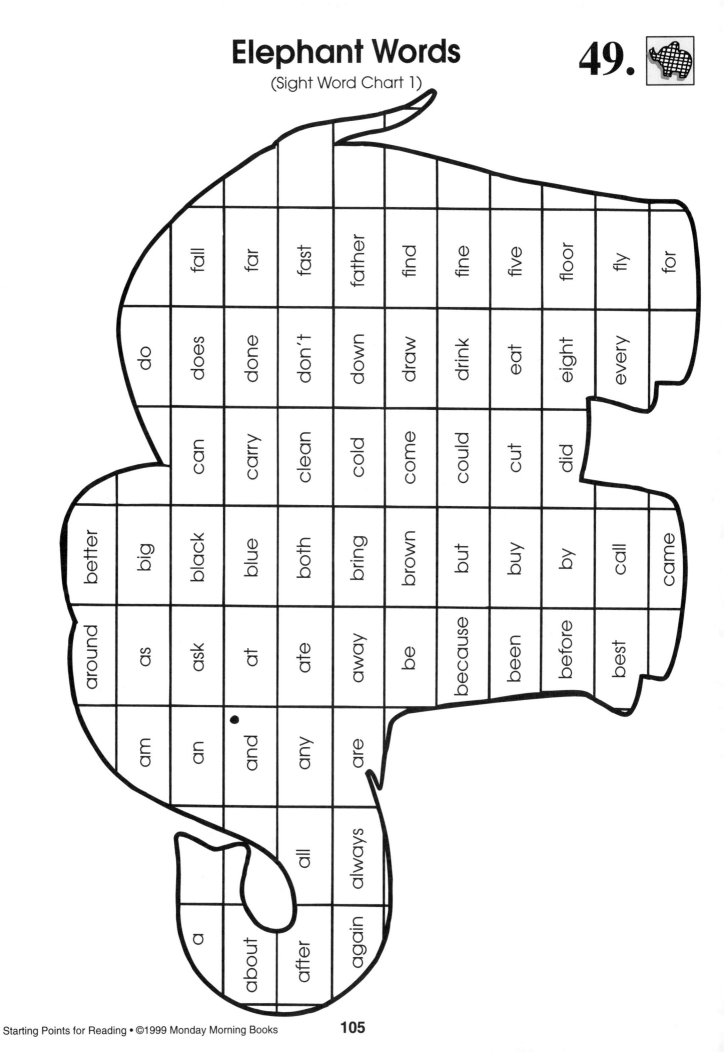

	fall	far	fast	father	find	fine	five	floor	fly	for
do	does	done	don't	down	draw	drink	eat	eight	every	
	can	carry	clean	cold	come	could	cut	did		
better	big	black	blue	both	bring	brown	but	buy	by	call	came
around	as	ask	at	ate	away	be	because	been	before	best
am	an	and	any	are						
		all	always							
a	about	after	again							

Hippo Words
(Sight Word Chart 2)

50.

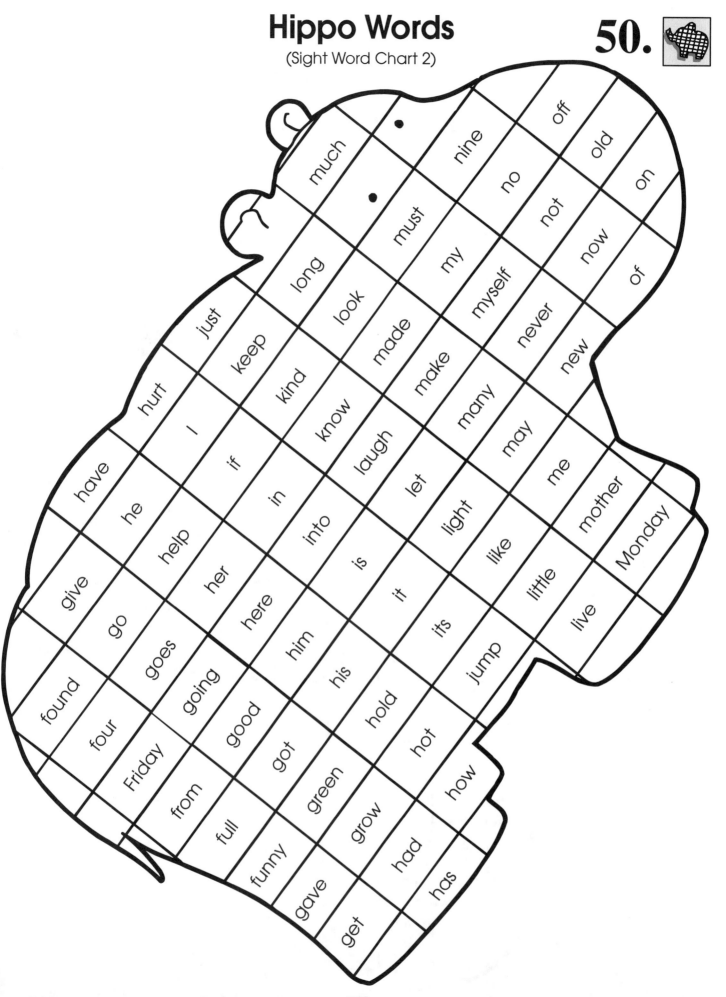

Bear Words
(Sight Word Chart 3)

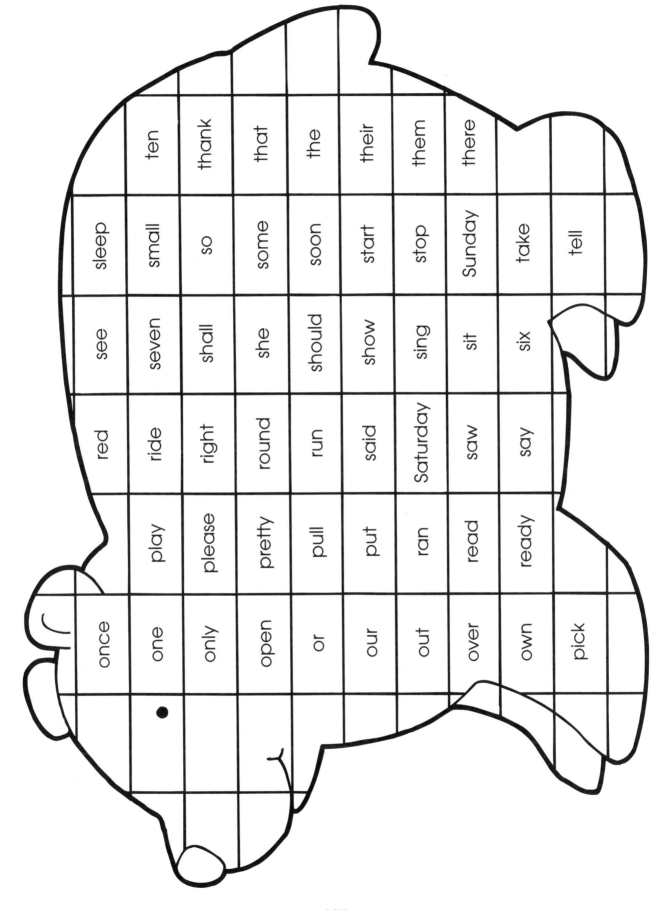

ten	thank	that	the	their	them	there
sleep	small	so	some	soon	start	stop	Sunday	take	tell
see	seven	shall	she	should	show	sing	sit	six
red	ride	right	round	run	said	Saturday	saw	say
play	please	pretty	pull	put	ran	read	ready
once	one	only	open	or	our	out	over	own	pick

Lion Words

(Sight Word Chart 4)

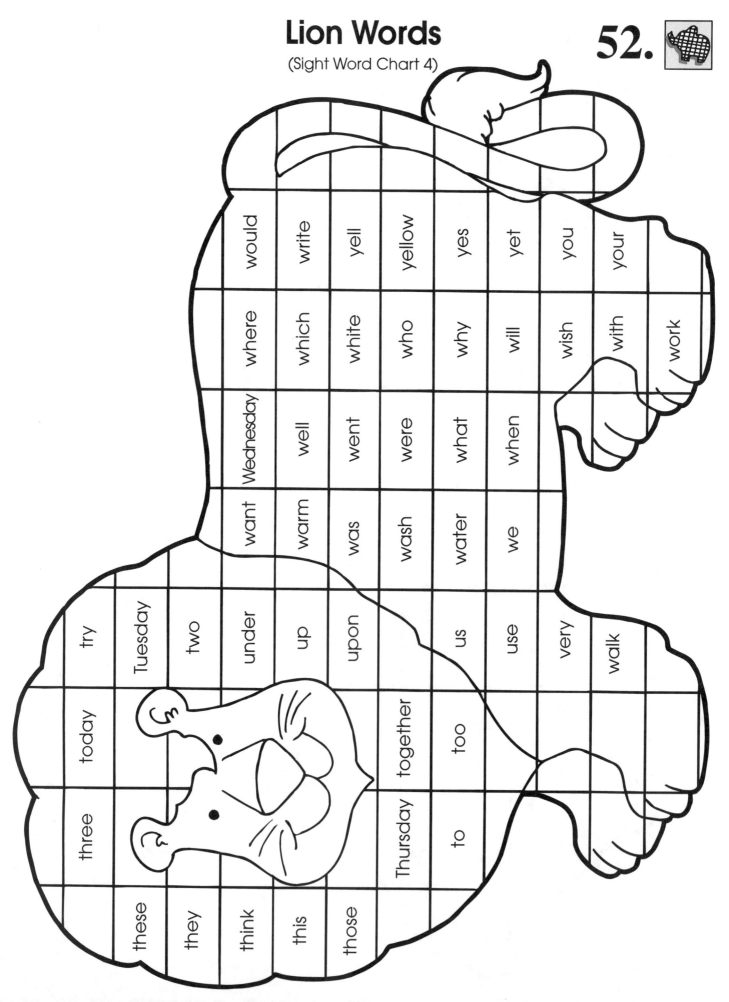

Sight Word Cards

a	are	before
about	around	best
after	as	better
again	ask	big
all	at	black
always	ate	blue
am	away	both
an	be	bring
and	because	brown
any	been	but

Sight Word Cards

buy	cut	eight
by	did	every
call	do	fall
came	does	far
can	done	fast
carry	don't	father
clean	down	find
cold	draw	fine
come	drink	five
could	eat	floor

Sight Word Cards

fly	give	have
for	go	he
found	goes	help
four	going	her
Friday	good	here
from	got	him
full	green	his
funny	grow	hold
gave	had	hot
get	has	how

Sight Word Cards

hurt	keep	look
I	kind	made
if	know	make
in	laugh	many
into	let	may
is	light	me
it	like	mother
its	little	Monday
jump	live	much
just	long	must

Sight Word Cards

my	old	own
myself	on	pick
never	once	play
new	one	please
nine	only	pretty
no	open	pull
not	or	put
now	our	ran
of	out	read
off	over	ready

Sight Word Cards

red	seven	so
ride	shall	some
right	she	soon
round	should	start
run	show	stop
said	sing	Sunday
Saturday	sit	take
saw	six	tell
say	sleep	ten
see	small	thank

Sight Word Cards

that	three	up
the	Thursday	upon
their	to	us
them	today	use
there	together	very
these	too	walk
they	try	want
think	Tuesday	warm
this	two	was
those	under	wash

Sight Word Cards

water	which	would
we	white	write
Wednesday	who	yell
well	why	yellow
went	will	yes
were	wish	yet
what	with	you
when	work	your
where		

Caterpillar Joe Goes on a Trip

Caterpillar Joe is on a trip.

1

He is on a big ship.

2

He has the best fun on the deck.

3

Caterpillar Joe Goes on a Trip

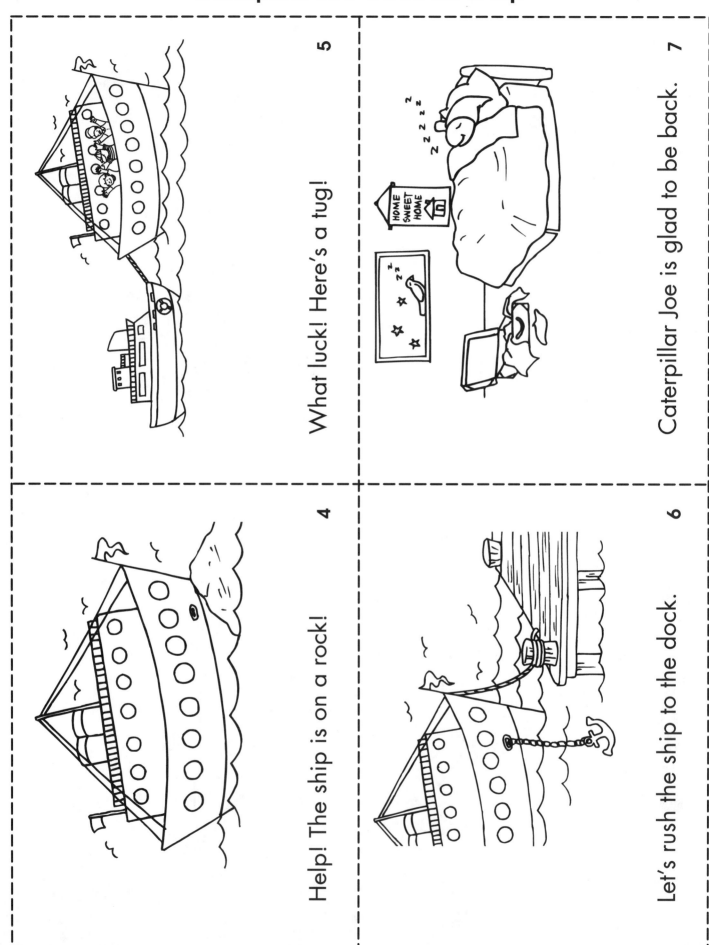

5

What luck! Here's a tug!

7

Caterpillar Joe is glad to be back.

4

Help! The ship is on a rock!

6

Let's rush the ship to the dock.

Caterpillar Joe's Garden

"What a good day to plant a garden," said Caterpillar Joe.

1

"Here are some seeds for you," said an odd little man. "Plant them when the moon is high."

3

He got out his rake, spade, and hoe. He dug and watered the soil.

2

Caterpillar Joe's Garden

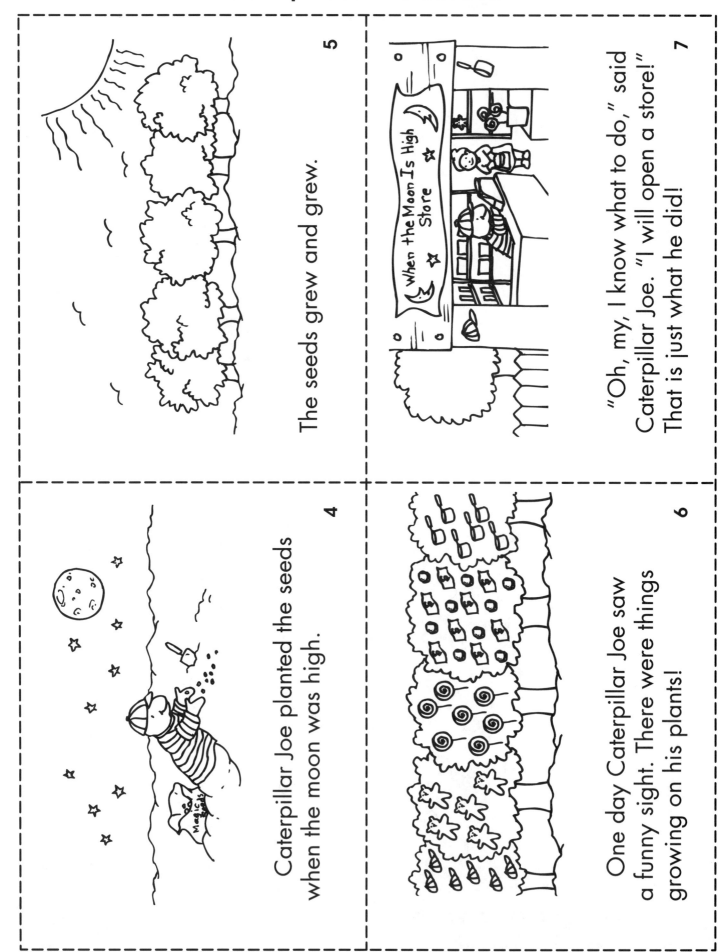

5

The seeds grew and grew.

7

"Oh, my, I know what to do," said Caterpillar Joe. "I will open a store! That is just what he did!

4

Caterpillar Joe planted the seeds when the moon was high.

6

One day Caterpillar Joe saw a funny sight. There were things growing on his plants!

1

Caterpillar Joe went to the pet store for some food for his pet fish. A little boy by the window asked, "Hey, mister, can I come in with you? Kids can't go in alone."

3

"Don't you have any pets?" asked Caterpillar Joe. "No, my mom and dad won't let me have one. They say they are a lot of trouble."

Caterpillar Joe's Good Deed

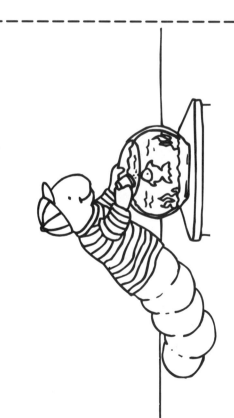

2

"Sure," said Caterpillar Joe. In the store, the boy looked at all the pets. "These pets are nice," he said sadly.

Caterpillar Joe's Good Deed

Hmm. A dog would chew up the chairs. A bird would drop seeds. A lizard would need fresh bugs. None of these pets would do.

5

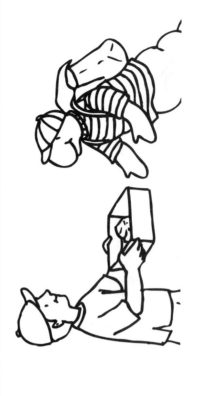

"Hey, mister, thanks! A pet rock!" cried the boy and ran off. In the box was a smooth black rock with a picture of a hamster.

7

Caterpillar Joe started to think. "What would be the best one for the little boy?" He looked all around the pet store.

Which pet?

4

Just then Caterpillar Joe spotted the best pet. He asked the store keeper to put it in a box. He gave it to the boy.

6

Caterpillar Joe Wins a Race

1

Caterpillar Joe is getting ready for the big triathlon race for bicycling, running, and swimming.

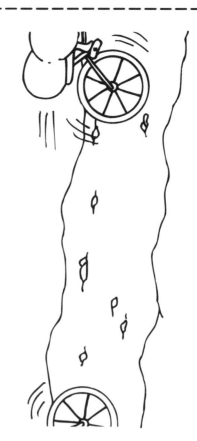

3

The big day is here. Caterpillar Joe gets a good start. He makes it over the tricky bicycle paths. He is ahead in the race!

2

He checks his bicycle to make sure it is in good shape. His running shoes are ready and his swimming goggles are packed.

Caterpillar Joe Wins a Race

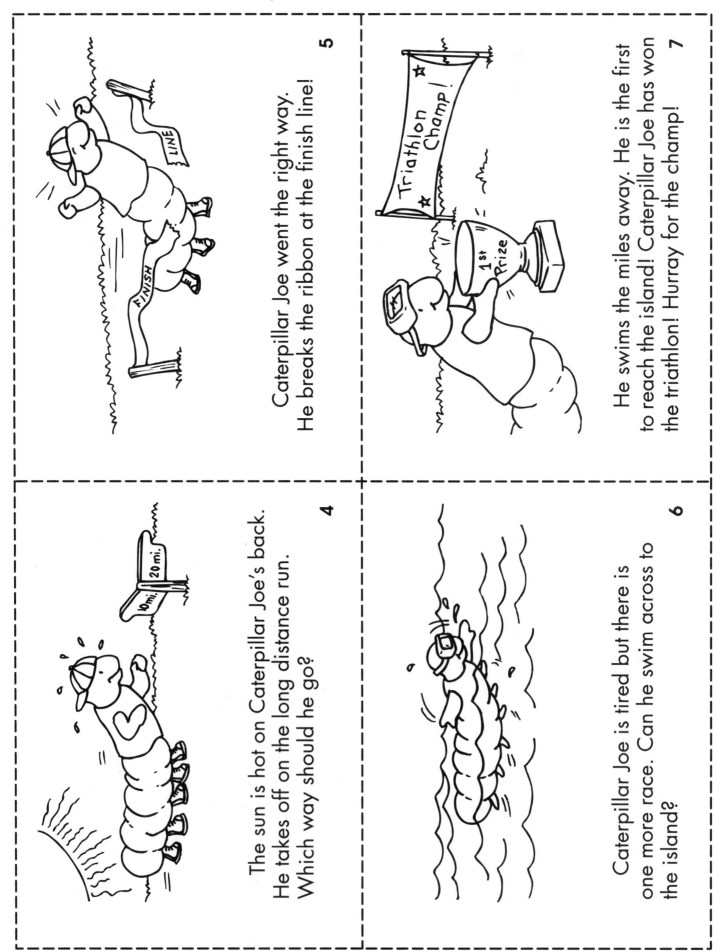

5

Caterpillar Joe went the right way.
He breaks the ribbon at the finish line!

7

He swims the miles away. He is the first
to reach the island! Caterpillar Joe has won
the triathlon! Hurray for the champ!

4

The sun is hot on Caterpillar Joe's back.
He takes off on the long distance run.
Which way should he go?

6

Caterpillar Joe is tired but there is
one more race. Can he swim across to
the island?

Caterpillar Joe Solves a Mystery

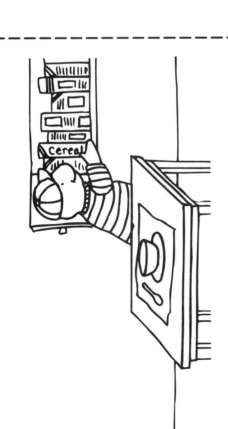

One morning, Caterpillar Joe sat down to eat his favorite cereal but the box was empty. Something had nibbled a big hole in the box. "I must find the culprit!" said Caterpillar Joe.

1

Caterpillar Joe looked for some clues. He checked the kitchen floor, table, and cupboards. Not a clue could he find.

2

"I know how I can catch this cereal robber!" thought Caterpillar Joe. That night, he carefully sprinkled some flour on the kitchen floor.

3

Caterpillar Joe Solves a Mystery

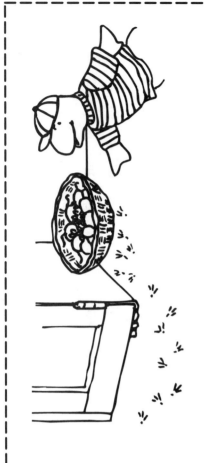

5

Caterpillar Joe opened the pantry door. There in a basket was not just one culprit but seven. A family of field mice, fast asleep!

7

Just to make sure of that, he left the field mice a big box of his favorite cereal!

4

In the morning, Caterpillar Joe crept into the kitchen. "Aha!" he said. "My plan worked!" Tiny, tiny tracks on the floor led to the pantry door.

6

"This will not do," said Caterpillar Joe. He put the field mice in a cage. He took them to a place where he knew they would have plenty to eat.

Caterpillar Joe Saves the Day

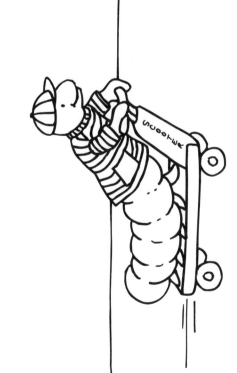

1

Here's Caterpillar Joe at the airport to greet the president of a big country. The president waves at the crowd.

2

Caterpillar Joe is the first to welcome the president. As the president shakes Joe's hand, something falls out of the president's pocket.

3

Fortunately, Caterpillar Joe picks it up. It is the president's speech! "I must get the speech to the president," says Caterpillar Joe. He jumps on his motor scooter and is off.

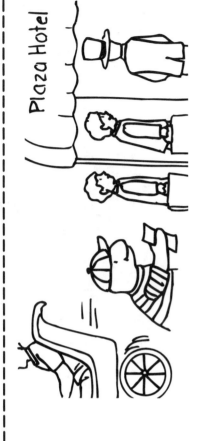

Plaza Hotel

Fortunately, Caterpillar Joe is able to get a free ride on a horse-drawn buggy. He sees the president enter the Plaza Hotel. Unfortunately, Caterpillar Joe is stopped at the door.

5

The president is delighted. He thanks Caterpillar Joe for his good deed. Caterpillar Joe has saved the president's day!

7

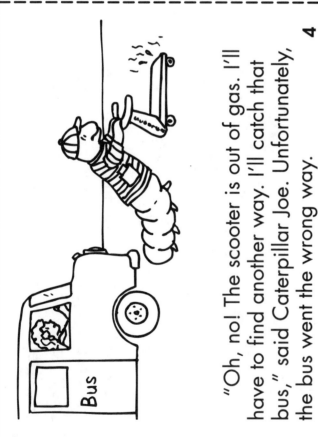

Bus

"Oh, no! The scooter is out of gas. I'll have to find another way. I'll catch that bus," said Caterpillar Joe. Unfortunately, the bus went the wrong way.

4

The president is ready to give his speech. He reaches into his pocket for the speech. It is not there! Fortunately, Caterpillar Joe rushes in and hands the president his speech.

6